Forget Baudrillard?

Edited by
Chris Rojek and Bryan S. Turner

London and New York

First published 1993
by Routledge
11 New Fetter Lane, London EC4P 4EE

Simultaneously published in the USA and Canada
by Routledge
29 West 35th Street, New York, NY 10001

Typeset in English Times by
Pat and Anne Murphy, Highcliffe-on-Sea, Dorset
Printed and bound in Great Britain by
Biddles Ltd, Guildford and King's Lynn

British Library Cataloguing in Publication Data
A catalogue record for this book is available from
the British Library.

Library of Congress Cataloging in Publication Data
Forget Baudrillard?/[edited by] Chris Rojek and Bryan S. Turner.
    p.   cm.
    Includes bibliographical references and index.
    1. Baudrillard, Jean.   2. Sociology – France – History.
    3. Sociology – Methodology.   4. Postmodernism – Social
aspects.
    I. Rojek, Chris.   II. Turner, Bryan S.
    HM22.F8B382   1993   93-14835
    301′.0944–dc20   CIP

    ISBN 0–415–05988–7 (hbk)
    ISBN 0–415–05989–5 (pbk)

'The road of excess leads to the palace of Wisdom.'
William Blake, *The Marriage of Heaven and Hell,*
Proverbs of Hell

'The book must break up so as to resemble the ever increasing number of extreme situations. It must break up to resemble the flashes of holograms. It must roll around itself like the snake on the mountains of the heavens. It must fade away as it is being read. It must laugh in its sleep. It must turn in its grave.'
Jean Baudrillard, *Cool Memories*

Forget Baudrillard?

Without doubt, Jean Baudrillard is one of the most important figures currently working in the area of sociology and cultural studies. But his writings infuriate as many people as they intoxicate. This collection provides a wide-ranging, measured assessment of Baudrillard's work. The contributors examine Baudrillard's relation to consumption, modernity, postmodernity, social theory, feminism, politics and culture. They attempt to steer a clear course between the hype which Baudrillard himself has done much to generate, and the solid value of his startling thoughts.

Baudrillard's ideas and style of expression provide a challenge to established academic ways of proceeding and thinking. The book explores this challenge and speculates on the reason for the extreme responses to Baudrillard's work. The appeal of Baudrillard's arguments is clearly discussed and his place in contemporary social theory is shrewdly assessed. Baudrillard emerges as a chameleon figure, but one who is obsessed with the central themes of style, hypocrisy, seduction, simulation and fatality. Although these themes abound in postmodern thought they are also evident in a certain strand of modernist thought – one which embraces the writings of Baudelaire and Nietzsche. Baudrillard's protestation that he is not a postmodernist is taken seriously in this collection.

The balanced and accessible style of the contributions and the fairness and rigour of the assessments make this book of pressing interest to students of sociology, philosophy and cultural studies.

Chris Rojek is Senior Editor in Sociology at Routledge and Visiting Fellow at the University of Portsmouth. **Bryan S. Turner** is Dean of Social Sciences at Deakin University, Australia.

Contents

Contributors

Zygmunt Bauman is Emeritus Professor in Sociology at the University of Leeds.

Dean MacCannell is Professor of Applied Behavioural Science and Sociology at the University of California, Davis.

Juliet Flower MacCannell is Professor of English and Director of the Program in Comparative Literature, University of California, Irvine.

Sadie Plant is Lecturer in Cultural Studies at the University of Birmingham.

Roy Porter is Senior Lecturer in the Social History of Medicine at the Wellcome Institute, London.

Chris Rojek is Senior Editor in Sociology at Routledge, London, and Visiting Fellow at the University of Portsmouth.

Barry Smart is Associate Professor in Sociology at the University of Auckland.

Bryan S. Turner is Dean of Social Sciences at Deakin University, Australia.

Introduction
Regret Baudrillard?

A recent review of one of Baudrillard's most important books, *Seduction*, illustrates the difficulty of commenting upon his work. The review, written by one of the shrewdest analysts of Baudrillard's œuvre,[1] begins by conveying the right air of gravitas. Baudrillard is described as a 'subtle', 'powerful' thinker. His work is considered to be at the cutting edge of social and cultural theory. However, quite quickly the reviewer is also driven to observe that many of Baudrillard's arguments are 'ludicrous'; and that his manner of presentation is often 'maladroit'. Yet the conclusion that one would predict from these serious criticisms is absent. We are *not* invited to reject Baudrillard. On the contrary he is presented as a figure of unique importance and his writing is recommended as required reading for anyone interested in current thought. 'Unsatisfactory as it obviously is,' writes Mike Gane (1992: 184) – the reviewer in question – 'unclassifiable as it is, it nevertheless throws up disturbing questions which will be dismissed only with a bad conscience.'

Gane's review illustrates why many academics find Baudrillard so perplexing. Elementary errors and wild arguments usually bring down the full weight of academic scorn. However, in Baudrillard's case they only seem to add to his charm. This is the writer who, among other things, has claimed blithely that America is utopia; that the masses have disappeared; that symbolic exchange is the only reality; and that the proper role for women is the role of the temptress. Baudrillard, it seems, gets away with murder.

The crabby response of the Academy is understandable. Much of academic life, like the world of theatre, is driven by resentment. Success and failure in academic careers are relatively public in terms of requests to appear on TV chat shows, to attend international conferences in desirable locations, or to have one's latest publication translated. There is also an important difference between France and Britain, in the sense that there is a very definite star-system among French academics. While Baudrillard might not be at the top of the French system, his rise to international fame has been quite spectacular. Here again, there is the irony of Baudrillard as an Event of Spectacle within the media scene of the Academy. Certainly Baudrillard must be offensive to those 'sound' academics who have not ventured outside the narrow confines of their specialism to speculate, without evidence, surveys, or confidence levels, on the meaning of Las Vegas or Reagan's face. It is interesting in this respect to compare Baudrillard with another global superstar, Umberto Eco. As far as we can tell, there has been no attempt to compare Baudrillard and Eco (Gane 1991a: 163). Both men have been fascinated by America, and particularly by the problem of reality/authenticity/hyperreality in American culture. Eco's book *Travels in Hyperreality* (1987) was originally published with the title *Faith in Fakes* (1986), although many of the first chapters first appeared in articles in Italian in the 1970s. Baudrillard's *America* (1988) first appeared in French as *Amérique* (1986). The parallels in time, titles and interests are striking. For Eco, American hyperreality has inauthenticated reality, creating a society with an addiction for fakes:

> This is the reason for this journey into hyperreality, in search of instances where the American imagination demands the real thing and, to attain it, must fabricate the absolute fake; where the boundaries between the game and illusion are blurred, the art museum is contaminated by the freak show, and falsehood is enjoyed in a situation of 'fullness', of *horror vacui*.
>
> (Eco 1987: 8)

Eco, who is world famous as the author of *The Name of the Rose*, is perhaps a more respectable figure than Baudrillard, because Eco continues to write 'serious scholarship', for example in the field of medieval theories of signs. Baudrillard's later work is increasingly cool.

Of course, the crabbiness against Baudrillard is not confined to academics used to the conventions of scholarly publication. Robert Hughes, the art critic of *Time* magazine is volcanically dismissive of Baudrillard's work. He (1990) ridicules the accuracy of Baudrillard's arguments on hyperreality, simulation and seduction. Hughes slightingly casts Baudrillard as an impressionable sensation-seeker, blind behind the astral wheel of mass culture. A casual reader may be forgiven for siding with Hughes. For Baudrillard's prose is inflated with outlandish confidence. Sometimes this can have unfortunate consequences. Thus, on the eve of the Geneva talks convened to avoid the Gulf War, Baudrillard could be found in the pages of *Libération* predicting that the Gulf War was impossible. Baudrillard argued that all of the permutations of war had been rehearsed by pundits and analysts on television. Therefore the real war can never happen because the phoney war has already been fought by the communications industry.

Baudrillard's recklessness may be criticized for undermining his credibility. However, perhaps he feels that this burden is bearable in a world which has, in his view, become totally artificial and parasitic. Simulation is the great theme in Baudrillard's writing. His definition of culture as 'the collective sharing of simulacra'[2] reduces truth and reality to a language game. Image makers have opened up a Pandora's box of illusions, treatments and enhancements which have obliterated the division between reality and unreality. Baudrillard's argument collides with most of the assumptions and conventions used to manage normality in everyday life. To many his analysis is literally out of this world. It is closer to the conventions of sci-fi than those of sociology. It is therefore perhaps appropriate to refer to an extra-terrestrial example to support Baudrillard's argument that the world is enwrapped in an epidemic of multiplying images which can only be described as 'hyperreality': 'the generation by models of a real without origin or reality' as Baudrillard (1983: 2) defines it. In April 1992 the London press ran stories of an image problem with the US space agency, NASA.[3] Scientists alleged that NASA's pictures of other worlds were being touched up. For example, the drab colours of the planet Mars and the asteroid Gaspara had been enhanced to become more vivid and spectacular. The Magellan probe which is now mapping the surface of the planet Venus has produced radar-controlled photographs which show towering volcanoes and bright yellow plains and mountains. However, radar cannot produce colour images. The yellow had been added by NASA imagineers. They are also alleged to have enhanced the size of the mountains of Venus by exaggerating the vertical planes of the photographs by a factor of 22. 'It's like playing with the control knobs on a television' commented astronomer Andrew Young of San Diego State University.

The example is not conclusive proof that Baudrillard is right.[4] However, it is symptomatic of the processes of simulation, seduction and hyperreality to which he returns repeatedly in his writings. This is appropriate. For does not Baudrillard fatalistically present himself as a symptom instead of a solution? His restless circling through the highways of America parallels the circlings of the sign in the sign economy. The sign economy is the sole universal recognized in Baudrillard's sociology. It is an encoded universe, a labyrinth, from which there is no escape. Baudrillard's fatalism is a notorious feature of his work. However few commentators have observed that it reveals a deeply conservative underbelly in his thought. For in Baudrillard's totally encoded universe it follows that any attempt to decode or manage things must be regarded with the utmost suspicion. It is no accident that Baudrillard's most recent book (1992) should use the metaphor of 'the orgy' to describe the 1960s. The New Left and feminist movements which emerged in those times aimed to change the world. Baudrillard's retrospective response is to note the fluid and brilliant patterns of encoding represented by the 1960s and to insist fastidiously upon their absolute uselessness.[5]

We have claimed that Baudrillard presents himself as a symptom, but a symptom of what? As with the last *fin de siècle* the 1990s are pregnant with uncertainty and awash with change. The eastern communist bloc collapses, but new ethnic conflicts break out from the Balkans to the Baltic. The global virus of AIDS introduces new doubts and fears into personal relationships. The global communications industry erodes traditional distinctions so that the difference between the local and the global becomes ever more ambiguous. The nation state in Europe seems to be in peril as pressure mounts from Brussels for European federation. Crime and murder seem to be on the increase. Political movements based in the principle of collective interest appear to have been bypassed by history. At such times, nervousness and anxiety are pronounced. Simmel (1990), of course, wrote about the neurasthenia of modern life at the turn of the century. He noted that in extreme cases it produced the pathologies of agoraphobia and hyperasthesia. More and more, argued Simmel, the individual is subjected to new stimulations and sensations, wild fluctuations in taste, style, opinions and personal relationships. The result, he concluded, is either the creation of the neurasthenic personality or the development of the blasé attitude which is based in total indifference and fatalism. Simmel was attacked by Lukács

(1991) and others for overemphasizing the haste and hurry of modern life and exaggerating the permanence of transitional forms of personal and social relationships. However this criticism was made before the two devastating world wars in Europe; before the Soviet road to communism was revealed to be a nightmare; and before the erosion of traditional family life. From the standpoint of the 1990s it is Simmel who looks if anything too conservative in his assessment of fragmentation, tumult and transition and his critics who look fooled by their own hyperbole.

Bauman (1987) divides intellectuals into legislators and interpreters. The legislators, he argues, aim to understand reality and lay down blueprints of change and improvement for society. In contrast, interpreters aim to translate meanings from one set of domain assumptions to another. The term 'domain assumptions' was coined by Gouldner (1971) to refer to the received opinions, beliefs and ideas underpinning a given system or social order. Interpreters seek to examine and communicate the gap between these domain assumptions and the trajectories of change experienced in society. On Bauman's distinction, Simmel is patently an interpreter, and so is Baudrillard. However, it would be rash to assume an evolutionary link between the two. Baudrillard is not the heir of Simmel. For one thing, Simmel retained the concept of the social. As a genuine *fin de millenium* and *fin de monde* figure Baudrillard argues that the social has imploded. In Simmel there is the acknowledgement of an emotional content to life, while in Baudrillard's media-fixated universe emotions have been neutralized by the blue glare of the TV screen. Yet both share a preference for a commentary which is phenomenologically grounded. Both react against approaches which view society or symbolic exchange as an object. There is an impressionistic quality to their writing which is perhaps inevitable in discussions which focus on change rather than order, becoming rather than being.

In his infamous squib, *Oublier Foucault* (1977)[6] Baudrillard goes further than anywhere else in his writing to disassociate himself from prevailing trends in social thought. Foucault is remorselessly attacked for giving misplaced concreteness to the concepts of power and repression. His 'histories' of madness, incarceration, medicalization and sexuality are castigated as confidence tricks which knowingly produce 'the effect of truth' while cynically harbouring no illusions that 'truth' is possible. Foucault is dismissed as a charlatan and necrophiliac, an *habitué* of the cadaverous sociology of structure, power and meaning. Against this Baudrillard does not proffer his own manifesto for 'sociology'.[7] Instead he allows certain values to come to the fore: mobility, dispersal, irony and scepticism. Although it is never stated directly the whole tenor of his criticism assumes that existence has moved on to a new stage which Foucault's traditional concepts of power, society and truth are incapable of grasping. Later, in *Cool Memories* (1990: 157–61) he argues that Foucault displayed traits of 'imperiousness' and 'despotism'. Traits which, Baudrillard continues, sprang from the cult which developed around Foucault and the idolatry of the spongers and hangers-on. It was not enough for Foucault to write about society; he also wanted society's approval. Baudrillard is of course implying that Foucault speared himself on the blade of his own naivety. The society to which Foucault ascribed solidity, weight, and depth is, for Baudrillard, elastic and transparent. But there is also in Baudrillard's vehemence a jarring streak of puritanism. He plainly abominates the Foucault fan club as much as he disapproves of Foucault's claim to have produced authoritative history. Vanities of any kind seem to offend this most whimsical of writers. However, the vanity of proclaiming an end to power, an end to society and an end to authority cannot have escaped Baudrillard's ironical mind. For these negations are unquestionably expressed in the tone of a writer who believes that he has something to say. Baudrillard writes with power and authority and always with an audience of readers in mind, a *social* grouping. Like Lyotard (1984) he preaches the death of meta-theory and meta-language, but in doing so he creates a new meta-theory and meta-language which is quite as enveloping and restrictive as the old.

Should we the regret the dazzling ascent of this writer in the Anglo-American world over the last decade? Certainly if the quality of a writer in the social sciences is to be assessed only by the validity of his or her propositions there is reason for regretting Baudrillard's success. Baudrillard has been wrong – spectacularly wrong – about a lot of things. One thinks of his prediction of the impossibility of the Gulf war; his assertion that America is already utopia; his reactionary thesis that the strength of the feminine is seduction; his eccentric defence of the concert against quadrophonic sound which is predicated in the argument that Mozart was never intended to be heard through electronic systems of reproduction; and his unsupported statement that the body has become a mere extension of network television. And one thinks of these things casually, without systematically sifting through the careening waves of Baudrillard's prose for other hostages to fortune or bad prophecies. In short, Baudrillard fails the validity test.

However, it is by no means clear that validity is the only or even the most important criterion to assess the significance of an author's work. Other criteria such as courage and sympathy are also relevant. In these respects Baudrillard is on stronger ground. The success of his publications in the English-speaking world since the 1980s suggests that his main themes of simulation and the seductiveness of consumer culture have found sympathy with a large audience of readers. Baudrillard may be wrong more often than he is right, but he has unquestionably struck the appropriate mood with which to approach questions of consumer culture. The subject of Baudrillard's courage has not been sufficiently profiled. Baudrillard's whimsical, unstructured publications are flagrantly antithetical to the dominant patterns of critical thought in the 1960s and 1970s. During this time varieties of scientific Marxism, cultural studies and structuralist feminism held the centre of the critical ground. Their popularity coincided with the expansion in higher education which established a secure institutional base for the promulgation of these views. Baudrillard does not use the term 'departmental fortresses' but it is quite apparent from his writing that he sees many social science departments as castles of engrained prejudice. None more so than those in which questions of class, patriarchy and hegemony are treated with a sort of ultimate authority and in which issues of simulation and seduction are treated as marginalia. Baudrillard's writing has, of course, enraged critics of this generation who accuse him of a lack of moral seriousness and irrelevance (see Callinicos 1989; Kellner 1989; Clarke 1991). But the very success of his work raises important questions about institutional closure within the Academy and the ossification of some influential traditions of critical thought.[8]

We have argued that Baudrillard is a controversial figure. Baudrillard provokes, unsettles, continues to annoy. In some respects, Baudrillard's style and impact are not unlike the Nietzsche of *The Gay Science*. Appropriately described as a 'prophet of extremity' (Megill 1985), Nietzsche questioned the taken-for-granted assumptions about the relationship between language and reality, mocked the respectable world of the German *Bildungs-bürgertum*, and adopted outrageous positions towards women, philosophers and full-time salaried academics. *The Gay Science*

(Nietzsche 1974), which is wonderfully rich in provocative meta-phors, maxims and morals, appeared in 1887. The word 'gay' in *Die Fröhliche Wissenschaft* might also be translated as 'joyful' or 'blithe', but these terms do not catch the feeling of exuberance in Nietzsche's language. Perhaps *Blissful Knowledge* might be a possible translation. Despite Baudrillard's interest in fatefulness, there is also an exuberant, playful, destructive aspect to Baudrillard's reflections on the simulations of the modern world. Perhaps Baudrillard's œuvre in respect might be regarded as a *fröhliche Theorie* as much as a fatal one.

This collection of essays does not settle the controversy. The Baudrillard that emerges from these pages is a combative, bom-bastic, shrewd, insightful and illogical commentator. The reader may be forgiven for concluding that the only consistent thing about him is his careless inconsistency. However, we are in no doubt that he is an important figure. Important not just in the mundane sense that many people are reading his publications and discussing his arguments, but important too in a strategic sense in that his approach and ideas expose the limitations of certain established ways of thinking about 'society', 'culture' and 'meaning'. Baudril-lard may not be the shape of things to come. Even so, perhaps more than any other contemporary writer he confronts the exhaustion of many of the guiding assumptions and beliefs that held critical thought together in the post-war period. So finally, he deserves the soubriquet given to him by *The New York Times*: 'a sharp-shooting lone ranger of the post-Marxist left'.

Chris Rojek, London
Bryan S. Turner, Wivenhoe
Winter 1993

NOTES

1 See Mike Gane (in *Theory Culture and Society* 9:2, May 1992, 183–4). Without doubt Mike is one of the best informed commentators on Baudrillard working in the English language. His two books (1991a, 1991b) on Baudrillard are essential reading for anyone seriously interested in Baudrillard and the relevant and historical contexts of his work.
2 As he (1990: 50) elaborates: 'culture has never been anything but . . . the collective sharing of simulacra, as opposed to the collective sharing of the real and meaning'. What price Marxism and feminism against this radical non-realist definition?

3 NASA is an acronym of the National Aeronautics and Space Adminis-
tration. Most of the factual details in our account of this image problem
come from the London *Observer*, 12 April 1992.

4 As many contributors to this book point out, if one follows Baudrillard's arguments about hyperreality and seduction, questions of right
and wrong, truth and fiction are meaningless.

5 One wonders if this was not also Baudrillard's response at the time.
There is in his writing the quality of the permanently detached spectator.
Baudrillard himself is fond of describing his work as the outpouring of
an outsider or misfit. While one can imagine his old collaborator Guy
Debord pitching himself into the fun and pranksterism of 1960s culture,
one can just as irresistibly picture Baudrillard participating peevishly and
sceptically.

6 Our own title is of course derived from this work. In Baudrillard's age of
simulation we thought it most appropriate to simulate his title, paying
due respect to his fondness for irony and double meaning.

7 The quotation marks are necessary because already in 1977, it is clear
that Baudrillard is uneasy with the term 'sociologist'. He taught
sociology at the University of Nanterre between 1966 and 1987. However, one suspects that he was never at ease with the subject. Perhaps it is
most accurate to describe Baudrillard's writing as 'commentary'.
Certainly the two travel diaries published in 1988 and 1990, namely,
America and *Cool Memories*, show no interest in matters of academic
regard.

8 We do not, of course, mean to suggest that Baudrillard has acted alone
in calling these traditions into question. On the contrary the 1980s wit-
nessed the emergence of a variety of 'post-Marxist' and 'post-feminist'
criticisms which are in no way compatible with the rule of capitalist
hegemony or the reproduction of patriarchal values. They just ask different questions – questions relating to the fragmentation, pluralism,
circulation and difference which have been marginalized by traditions
which take 'the class struggle' or 'the universal experience of women' as
their foundation. For a discussion of processes of closure within the
English intelligentsia see Turner (1992).

REFERENCES

Baudrillard, J. (1977) *Oublier Foucault*, Paris, Galilée.
—— (1983) *Simulations*, New York, Semiotext(e).
—— (1988) *America*, London, Verso.
—— (1990) *Cool Memories*, London, Verso.
—— (1992) *The Transparency of Evil*, London, Verso.
Bauman, Z. (1987) *Legislator and Interpreters*, Cambridge, Polity Press.
Callinicos, A. (1989) *Against Postmodernism: A Marxist Critique*,
Cambridge, Polity Press.
Clarke, J. (1991) *New Times, Old Enemies*, London, HarperCollins.
Eco, U. (1987) *Travels in Hyperreality*, London, Picador (*Faith In Fakes*,
London, Secker and Warburg, 1986).

Gane, M. (1991a) *Baudrillard: Critical and Fatal Theory*, London, Routledge.

—— (1991b) *Baudrillard's Bestiary*, London, Routledge.

—— (1992) Review of Baudrillard, J., *Seduction* in *Theory, Culture and Society* 9(2), 183–4.

Gouldner, A. (1971) *The Coming Crisis of Western Sociology*, London, Heinemann.

Hughes, R. (1990) *Nothing if not Critical*, London, Harvill/HarperCollins.

Kellner, D. (1989) *Jean Baudrillard*, Cambridge, Polity Press.

Lukács, G. (1991) 'George Simmel', *Theory, Culture and Society* 8(3), 145–50.

Lyotard, J. (1984) *The Postmodern Condition*, Manchester, MUP.

Megill, A. (1985) *Prophets of Extremity, Nietzsche, Heidegger, Foucault, Derrida*, Berkeley, University of California Press.

Nietzsche, F. (1974) *The Gay Science*, New York, Vintage.

Simmel, G. (1990) *The Philosophy of Money*, London, Routledge.

Turner, B. S. (1992) 'Ideology and Utopia in the formation of an intelligentsia: Reflections on the English cultural conduit', *Theory, Culture and Society* 9(1), 183–210.

Chapter 1

Baudrillard: history, hysteria and consumption

Roy Porter

'Signs, signs? Is that all you have to say?'

In a powerful maturation of thought, first discernible in works such as *Le Système des objets* (1968) and *La Société de consommation* (1970) and culminating in *L'Echange symbolique et la mort* (1976) and *Simulations* (1981), Jean Baudrillard came to argue that a key characteristic of the contemporary world is that previously stable socioeconomic categories, notions like value and need, have lost their inherent meaning and objective anchorage.[1] Classical political economy posited such elements as independently determined; market forces might change their balance, but the pitch was clearly chalked out and the goalposts fixed. Capitalism, according to standard treatises, was a system of commodity production; value was produced by the labour (power) essential to manufacture; through the play of market forces, output responded to consumer demand, and demand was a function of need. There were iron laws of political economy, grounded in nature (the material world, natural need, the laws of utility), and known by science. Free-marketeers and Marxists might argue over the details, but the rules of the game – secular fluctuations of rate of profit, and so forth – were agreed touchstones.[2]

The modern consumer society is another beast. It is, Baudrillard claimed, a system in which analysis of the laws of production has become obsolete. Consumption is all-important, and consumption has to be understood in a novel manner. Thanks to the twentieth-century revolutionization of consciousness – through mass communications, hi-tech media, the advertising and publicity industries, the empire of images throughout the global village – modern human beings now inhabit an artificial, hermetically sealed pleasure dome. [Nothing is constant, everything reflects everything else in a theatre of dazzling simulations dominated by the proliferation of the sign and manipulated by ever-hidden persuaders.] Desire itself is manufactured, and nothing any longer possesses intrinsic value, in and for itself. Meaning is produced by endless, symbolic exchanges within a dominant code, whose rhetoric is entirely self-referential; a sexy woman is used to sell a car; a car sells cigarettes; cigarettes sell machismo; machismo is used to sell jeans; and so the symbolic magic circle is sealed. Sex, youth, health, speed, style, power, money, mobility – all transvalue and interpenetrate in the mesmerizing dreamworld of 'floating signifiers' that typifies the ephemeral, destabilized vortex of late capitalism. Baudrillard likens such dizzying, ever-repeated, and omni-purpose emblems to the symptoms of hysteria:

> The world of objects and of needs would thus be a world of *general hysteria*. Just as the organs and the functions of the body in hysterical conversion become a gigantic paradigm which the symptom replaces and refers to, in consumption objects become a vast paradigm designating another language through which something else speaks.[3]

I find this allusion to 'hysteria' a singularly apt figure of speech, for a variety of reasons that I shall explore below. For one thing, semiologically speaking, both classical hysteria and modern capitalism evoke an intense, slippery, baffling network of fleeting, volatile manifestations (erratic pains, seizures, highs and depression in the individual; or crazes, fashions, publicity hypes, crises and crashes in the body politico-economic) which possibly serve as teasing surrogates for the underlying reality, or more likely mask an absence, a void, beneath and within.[4] As hysteria (or, as was sometimes said, 'mysteria') was often regarded as artifice, mimicry or malingering, or at best a trick of the psyche, so in contemporary capitalism, the measure of 'health', as recorded, say, by the Dow-Jones or FT index, is essentially nominal or 'paper', a token of self-induced confidence or panic. Hysteria in *fin de siècle* Vienna or Paris was not, in truth, an underlying disease but a script, a theatre of display, focused upon *conversion*; so, in a similar manner, modern capitalism deploys its own alchemy, depending on the blinding spectacle of high-speed circulation. The grand economic conjuring trick requires that all balls be kept moving, at high velocity, through the air at once; once one crashes to the ground, *lo spettacolo è finito*.

Baudrillard thus invites diagnosis of late capitalism as frenzied, hectic, morbid. And the hysteria metaphor serves a further purpose. It draws attention to the ways in which both the hysterical body and the capitalist exchange system defy the analytic cage dictated by the seventeenth-century philosophical revolution, brought in by the New Science with all the epistemological, ontological and methodological entailments that deemed reality mechanical and grounded words in things. In the very thick of that revolution, hysteria was the sly imp that thumbed its nose and poked out its tongue at the neat Cartesian mind–body dualism; hysteria mocked the formally clear-cut boundaries delineating soma from psyche, the physical from the moral, malady from malevolence. The market economy similarly proved a will-o'-the-wisp. From the seventeenth century, a succession of illustrious thinkers claimed that analysis of wealth must become a sister discipline to the natural sciences, an objective, dispassionate investigation of regular motions and exchanges, reducible to natural laws, expressible in numerals, algebra, equations, capturing the behaviour of *Homo oeconomicus*, that most regular of guys. Yet, 300 years later, the economy remains altogether fetishized and treated anthropomorphically: yesterday (we say) it was healthy, today it may be somewhat weaker, but hopefully, tomorrow, it will rally and make a complete recovery, perhaps by shedding some surplus fat, growing lean and fit. By designating the economy as hysterical, Baudrillard forces us to examine our presuppositions about the march of western rationality. Entities which are supposed to have been subject to Weberian 'demystification', constituting value-free objects of disinterested scientific enquiry, still seem to possess, by some magic, a sneaky life of their own. Clearly, Baudrillard is implying, we must think of economic activity as proceeding not in a laboratory but in a theatre.[5] We are indoctrinated into a body of teaching that explains the growing scientificity of western understanding of the laws of capital, and the emplacement, down the centuries, of an ever more rational order for the expediting of enterprise and the unbinding of Prometheus.[6] But Whiggish myth and mystification lurk here. Scrutiny of the fine texture of political economy down the centuries shows it always has been – and still is – saturated with concepts and rhetoric appropriated and absorbed from a welter of other thought-worlds: physiology, medicine, psychology, geography, philology, ethics, divinity, and so forth.[7] For example, the advocacy of the free market by the devotees of Adam Smith hinged upon a medical analogue: the brisk, free circulation of capital was as essential as the unimpeded circulation of blood or 'animal spirits' within the 'animal economy'.[8] In later economic thought, the self-adjusting quality of mature capitalism was often compared to the homoeostatic mechanisms of the living form.[9] By invoking the hysterical body, Baudrillard thus defies the received truth that the economic domain belongs to the supposedly value-neutral realm of natural science, challenges the privileging of the economic, and re-alerts us to the ubiquitous role of language, symbol and rhetoric in the constitution of meaning.

Baudrillard's account of the hysteria of late capitalism would, in many respects, have made perfect sense to Freud and all the other eminent *fin de siècle* diagnosticians of civilization and its discontents.[10] As has been especially well documented by Rosalind Williams, late nineteenth-century critics became preoccupied with exhaustion and the enervation consequent upon the incessant movement of urban life and 'image overload'.[11] With their explosion of magazines and mass communications, their department stores and world fairs, their saturation advertising, their cornucopia of consumer merchandise and the surrounding hullabaloo of junk publicity, their technological novelties and their obligatory, upbeat public frivolity, late nineteenth-century New York or London, Paris or Vienna were widely seen by critics as health hazards, endangering the moths irresistibly attracted to the incandescent glow of commerce. Such worlds of fascination, bright lights, electric sound, and dazzling night-life were almost tailor-made to bring forth the newly diagnosed disorder of mass hysteria.[12] Laying bare the interconnections between economics, sexology, and psychology, Lawrence Birken has stressed how Freud analysed the enforced sublimation of primary sexual desires into the texture of civilization: art, religion, and advanced capitalism's 'world of goods'. Precious material objects, like jewels and jewel cases, figure time and again in Freud's case studies as sexual surrogates. It was, we might say, indicative of the hysterical aura of bourgeois mores that a certain level of sexual abstinence was mandatory in a material economy in which nothing was denied. Sex was kept a scarce commodity to hold its value up. With free trade in goods coexistent with protectionism in libidinal exchange, there was a confusion of codes that engendered hysteria.[13]

Sexual scarcity in part explains Freud's gloominess about the human condition under advanced capitalism. Something else fuelled the pessimism of Freud and other contemporary physician–critics: the fear that the acceleration of living characteristic of the ages of steam and electricity was imposing insupportable demands upon the human body and mind. The neurotics, neuropaths and neurasthenics who crawled up the stairs of Berggasse 19 in Vienna or visited divers other psychiatric clinics in Berlin, Zurich and Paris were suffering, it was agreed, from fatigue and lassitude. Exhausted nerves were a *Zeitgeist* disease. As Francis Gosling and Tom Lutz have shown, the disease had spread to the New World too. Illustrious American nerve-doctors like George Beard and Weir Mitchell argued that career strains in the business rat race devitalized high-flyers; brain-fagged by stress and tension in the cockpit of commerce, they cracked, ending up nervous wrecks, their psychological capital overtaxed. Cerebral circuits suffered overload, mental machinery blew fuses, batteries ran down, brains were bankrupted. Such metaphors, borrowed from physics and engineering, show once again the interdependence of the image worlds of biomedicine, economics and science: M. E., or chronic fatigue syndrome, by-products amongst yuppies of the Reaganite and Thatcherite 'greed is good' gospels of the 1980s, suggest yet a further case of old wine in new bottles, *plus ça change, plus c'est la même chose.*[14] 'What is hanging over us now', reflects the jaded Baudrillard of the 1980s, 'is not hysteria or schizophrenia . . . but . . . melancholia. With its precursor, hypochondria, that derisory signalling of overcathected, enervated bodies and organs, rendered sad by involution. All systems, especially political ones, are virtually hypochondrial: they manage and ingest their own dead organs.'[15]

Baudrillard depicts the contemporary capitalist body politic as hyperkinetic. Everything tingles, radiates, reverberates. All is in flux, everything is reflected or refracted through various media, speed is hypnotic, there is a carnival of hyperreal appearances, an appetite for excitement. The advent of what Marcuse dubbed 'repressive desublimation', releasing a long repressed libidinal hedonism in a shout of 'I want it now', produces a hyperaesthetized mass hysteria throughout the body politico-economic, a multi-media whirl of 'floating signifiers'.

Baudrillard offers an evocative, if impressionistic, picture of contemporary capitalism. What needs to be emphasized from the historical viewpoint is that this characterization of capitalism as a fevered, frenzied epidemic of signs is not applicable solely to *late* capitalism. At least since the seventeenth century, capitalism has been inseparable from the incitement of imagination, the creation of blitzes of speculation, fantasy, fiction, hyperstimulation – and from the attendant destabilizing mental and emotional disturbances. In saying this I may be parting company with Baudrillard himself. For in various places[16] he sketches, perhaps nostalgically, a world we have lost in which signifiers, signified and referents formerly appear to have been healthily cemented together. The Renaissance believed in the cosmic match of *res et verbum*. The Enlightenment asserted its faith in a foundational plain-dealing nature. There must be no magical signs; all valid signs must relate back to nature. It is with the twentieth-century media explosion and the dominance of the masses that things have radically changed.

There is an element of truth in such a view. There is, furthermore, an appealing logic in a metanarrative which would relate the rise of free-market, commercial and industrial capitalism on the basis of rock-solid 'realities' – superior capital investment, technological breakthroughs, the recruitment of proletarianized labour, unlimited expansion of output, the globalization of the market and so forth. Capitalism had thus (in this saga) proceeded 'rationally' – until, that is, at some negotiable crisis-or-transition-point, it had transformed itself, thanks to Madison Avenue and Hollywood, television and videos, into an irrational 'dream' economy, buoyed up by the big lie, by fantasies and the fabrication of spurious desires. Such a legend could coincide nicely with scenarios variously peddled for capitalism's future. In any case, there are manifest attractions to construing our own times as unique: uniquely exciting, uniquely depressing. My point, however, is that an adequate understanding of the historical dynamics of capitalism requires that we also analyse its early development, in terms similar to those Baudrillard might reserve for contemporary times.

In the early centuries of capitalism, the discourse of wealth was never seen as an exclusive matter of rational, utilitarian maximization. Opulence was always regarded as integral to broader moral and cosmic questions of order, harmony, balance, teleology, and health in its widest sense. 'What makes a commonwealth prosper?', asked the political thinkers of early modern times. Obviously, the body politic had to be kept from wasting away: national poverty was symptomatic of broken constitutions, a recipe for internal disorder and dynastic weakness alike. National strength had to be consolidated, through riches and populousness. Yet plenty too held its dangers. Muscle readily ran to fat, and the corpulence of state was all too often maldistributed: everyone knew that the head and belly – courts and 'corporations' – engorged themselves at the expense of the true sinews of the state (above all, the 'hands'), organs in danger of withering away.[17]

As the lifeblood or vital spirits of the incorporated nation, the function of wealth was to flow. Rejecting old-fashioned 'bullionism', the miser's dream that treasure lay in hoarded gold and silver, seventeenth-century analysts promoted the more refined view that true wealth sprang from money in motion, stimulating labour, industry and exchange. William Harvey's discovery of the circulation of the blood perhaps underwrote the mercantilist credo that well-being stemmed from the velocity and quantity of commercial transactions. Even then, prescribing the right regimen for the body politic was a perplexing policy matter. Immoderate wealth, love of lucre and luxury, so prestigious religious and moral teachings warned, were the cancers of the commonwealth. Mercantilism itself, philosophically inclined to saving rather than spending, feared affluence would be squandered on dross, for what was expenditure but 'spending', the dissipation of accumulated resources? Conspicuous consumption was conspicuous waste.[18] If production was the *summum bonum* for early wealth theorists, consumption was their headache. For the notion of consumption triggered innumerable semantic and semiotic ambiguities, suggesting both an enlargement through incorporation, and a withering away, both enrichment and impoverishment. Moreover, alongside its politico-economic meanings, 'consumption' carried a specific medical connotation: the wasting disease we call tuberculosis which became one of the greatest scourges of the period after 1700.[19] A terrible paradox had emerged within the language field, but also the realities, of economics. On the one hand, it could be axiomatic for Adam Smith, that the end of all economic activity was consumption; yet, semantically and symbolically, consumption was a disease, a disease of waste; while, at the same time, another mode of analysis that crystallized in Ricardo was apprehensive that the iron law of wages and the operation of boundless competition were bringing about a stalling economy undermined by 'underconsumption'. Consumption was clearly the sphinxian riddle of early modern economics.

The paradox and the pathology of consumption were particularly neatly pinpointed by Thomas Beddoes, the Bristol physician and political radical, active at the close of the eighteenth century, and a specialist in tuberculosis. Beddoes noted the vast expansion of free market activity in his day: 'In the social arrangements which have gradually formed themselves in Europe,' he observed, 'WEALTH, the most general object of power, becomes the most general object of desire.'[20] A restless, mobile emulative, achiever society, marked by new urban conveniences, domestic luxuries, and greater freedom of lifestyle ('in no country is there so large a proportion of inhabitants with such liberty of choice, as in Great Britain'),[21] was evidently emerging, thanks in part to an explosion of signs: in Beddoes's view, much of the commerce of his day was the commerce in ideas, images, ideologies, materialized by the programme of the Enlightenment and the advent of newspapers, magazines, novels and public opinion.[22] An air of artifice had been created in polite society, unsettling, dislocating; economically uncertain ('Is all this [progress] solid benefit or empty boast?') and psychologically disturbing, perhaps presaging an imminent 'millennium of misery'?[23]

Hectic change threatened economic and personal health alike. Producers suffered: 'The encouragement of manufactures', he quipped, 'is the creation of a miserable and sickly population'.[24] But the consuming classes were victims of their own cravings. Money was a devil that drove its votaries to distraction. 'Go for instance to the scenes of trade at London or at Bristol', Beddoes urged:

> Among the faces that appear at high 'Change, mark those that bespeak the cares attendant upon wealth already accumulated; and those others, where an added air of wildness characterises the speculator, too much in haste to wait for the reward of regular industry, and burning to get rich by the lucky hit. Some of these men will grow mad enough to be watched at home or sent to a lunatic asylum, where they will be haunted by the fear of coming upon the parish.[25]

And money madness imperilled not only yuppie speculators but the 'opportunity society' at large.[26] 'The universal facility of credit in this country', Beddoes alleged, was often disastrous for health, especially for 'those students who are in haste to ruin their constitution'. Easy come, easy go: credit today, the clink tomorrow. *'All the world is melancholy, because all the world is in debt'* – this commonplace 'observation', he reflected, 'certainly, will not account for the whole of the melancholy among us . . . But it will account for a great many of those unwelcome visitations, against which no gaiety of apparel is able to protect many a snowy bosom'.[27]

And alongside the hysteria of commercial capitalism, its laws of consumption were spreading the organic disease, consumption. Tuberculosis had become rampant amongst factory hands living in the jerry-built slums of the new manufacturing towns. But it was also the disease of the fashionable – indeed a *fashionable* disease, amongst those addicted to new skimpy sartorial fashions, enslaved to exquisite sensibility, and hooked on the new crazes for languor, thinness, and vegetarianism.

A further perspective on consumption is afforded by Beddoes's exact contemporary, the Scottish-born naval physician, Thomas Trotter. In his *Essay . . . on Drunkenness* (1804), and his *View of the Nervous Temperament* (1807), Trotter argued that:

> The last century has been remarkable for the increase of a class of diseases, but little known in former times, and what had slightly engaged the study of physicians prior to that period. They have been designated in common language, by the terms NERVOUS; SPASMODIC; BILIOUS; INDIGESTION; STOMACH COMPLAINTS; LOW SPIRITS; VAPOURS, &c.[28]

Nervous disorders were in a very direct manner the diseases of the consumer society, for many of the key items of soaring consumption were drugs, narcotics, or addictive substances – notably tea, coffee, strong liquor, tobacco, opium, patent medicines (we might almost say, 'designer drugs') – which transfixed their victims in ever more terrifying spirals of psychedelic consumption. Referring back to the 'from rudeness to refinement' socioeconomic philosophy developed in the Scottish Enlightenment, Trotter offered a metanarrative in which the rude health of peasants typical of traditional rural life had been exchanged for disease in the milieu of the city, where humankind had become 'the creature of art', and the mirage of progress fomented a spirit of inquietude, a restless, insatiable quest for faddish gratifications, wilder excitements, 'excessive stimuli' and 'debilitating pleasures'.[29] And if, in Trotter's moral vision, capitalist exchange in the kaleidoscopic environment of the city had produced enslavement to consumption, had made people slaves to objects of desire, a further contemporary underlined the dangers posed by desire for the equipoise of capitalism. In his *Essay on Population* (1798), the Revd Thomas Malthus argued that agricultural production could not keep up with the demand for food created by the force of sexual desire amongst the labouring classes. As Catherine Gallagher has justly observed, by insisting on the bio-sexual medical aspect of production/reproduction, Malthus upset the classical economics applecart.[30] In short, we cannot understand the logic of political economy in the age of Smithian economics except by exploring the polysemic and contested meanings of its central concepts.

Through these brief examples, I have been contending that, even in its golden age, the free market economic defies analysis in terms of utilitarian measures of rationality. *Homo œconomicus* was always also *le malade imaginaire*, *Homo hystericus*, *Homo gulosus*, and so forth.

The same is true if we finally return to what is commonly regarded as the decisive period in the making of commercial capitalism and the formative years of liberal political economy, the last decades of the seventeenth century. Here 'hysteria' becomes particularly relevant.

In radically contrasting historiographies, hysteria has been respectively represented as, according to Ilza Veith, a perennial disease, present since the Pharaohs, and, in Thomas Szasz's view, a 'myth' invented by Freud to serve the mission of psychoanalysis.[31] A more historicallly sensitive reading, however, shows that, as a diagnostic category, 'hysteria' came into common use in the early modern era, to depict a strange malady, with fleeting symptoms that had once largely been attributed either to demonic possession or to the 'wandering womb'. Now it was increasingly seen as a 'nervous' complaint, and it was reckoned to be spreading. The great Restoration clinician, Thomas Sydenham, thought 'of all chronic diseases hysteria – unless I err – is the commonest'.[32] It was peculiarly protean and labile – 'this disease', Sydenham stressed, 'is not more remarkable for its frequency, than for the numerous forms under which it appears, resembling most of the distempers wherewith mankind are affflicted' – but it largely struck down the affluent, being apparent amongst both men and women, especially 'such male subjects as lead a sedentary or studious life, and grow pale over their books and papers'.[33] If every age gets the diseases it deserves, surely it can be no accident that hysteria assumed centre-stage in an era of spiralling wealth, urban growth, commercial development, the age which saw the rise in the Netherlands and Britain, of banking and brokerage, speculation and stock exchanges, the flotation of new currencies, a fashionable unsettling individualism and liberty in politics and religion, thought and publishing. It seemed to many critics a world run riot with unrealities: paper money, inflation, the debasement of the currency, wigs, vizards, the masquerade and other forms of make-up. The logical, melancholy consequence of this pursuit of make-believe was the South Sea Bubble, the epitome of speculative madness, a delusion, a fiction, a sickness of state, leading to a multitude of suicides and madnesses: such at least was the observation of many critics, not least J. Midriff's *Observations on the Spleen and Vapours, Containing Remarkable Cases of Persons of Both Sexes and All Ranks from the Aspiring Directors in the Humble Bubbler who have been Miserably Afflicted with these Melancholy Disorders Since the Fall of the South Sea and Other Public Stocks* (1721).[34]

The disease of affluence was diagnosed in one of the most influential medico-critical works of the early Georgian era, George Cheyne's *The English Malady*. A fashionable Bath and London physician, Cheyne argued that the consuming classes would inevitably suffer from nervous and hysterical conditions, because they were living in the tinsel whirl of polite society, deranged by excess stimuli. Cheyne offered a primitivist tale of the psyche becoming crazed and broken by the pressures of commercial civilization. 'When Mankind was simple, plain, honest and frugal, there were few or no diseases. Temperance, Exercise, Hunting, Labour, and Industry kept the Juices Sweet and the Solids brac'd.'[35] As early as ancient civilization, however, the rot had set in. The Greeks were conveniently praised for inventing medicine. But had they not been *driven* to it by the proliferation of sickness caused by their softened, sedentary, urban existence? Thereafter it was downhill all the way. Prosperous England was now suffering actutely from the pangs of prosperity:

> Since our Wealth has increas'd, and our Navigation has been extended, we have ransack'd all the Parts of the *Globe* to bring together its whole Stock of Materials for *Riot*, *Luxury*, and to provoke *Excess*.[36]

The various elements of England's commercial and social success were now conspiring to maximize sickness:

> *The* Moisture *of our* Air, *the Variableness of our* Weather, *(from our Situation amidst the* Ocean) *the* Rankness *and* Fertility

of our Soil, the Richness *and* Heaviness *of our Food, the* Wealth *and* Abundance *of the Inhabitants (from their universal Trade) the* Inactivity *and* Sedentary *Occupations of the better Sort (amongst whom this* Evil *mostly rages) and the Humour of living in great, populous and consequently unhealthy Towns, have brought forth a* Class *and* Set *of Distempers, with atrocious and frightful* Symptoms, *scarce known to our Ancestors, and never rising to such fatal* Heights, *nor afflicting such* Numbers *in any other known Nation.*[37]

Cheyne argued that fast-lane living in trendy commercial society required the successful to be feverishly productive in wit, ideas, and social invention. The glitterati were thus forced to have recourse to the stimulus of food and drink. Overconsumption, anxiety, speculation and sedentary habits triggered nervous diseases, hysteria and hypochondria: 'These monstrous and extreme *Tortures*, are entirely the Growth of our own Madness and Folly, and the Product of our own wretched Inventions.'[38] Cheyne's linking of fashionable society and fashionable diseases was driven home by a somewhat later Bath physician, Dr James McKitrick Adair. In his *Essays on Fashionable Disorders* (1790), Adair lamented that medicine had been sucked into the maelstrom of modishness, which 'like its companion Luxury, may be considered as one of those excrescences which are attached to national improvement'.[39] The Janus face of fashion was, doubtless, the key to the civilizing process: 'as societies advance in civilization, the active mind of man, not contented with the means of satisfying our natural wants, is anxiously employed in creating artificial wants, and inventing the means of their gratification', the consequence being the 'empire of fashion'.[40] Fashion's sway had 'now become universal; it is not confined to the decorations of our persons, or the embellishment of our houses and equipages; but extends to our politics, morals, religion, and even in some degree to our sciences'. Even medicine, he regretted, 'is become subject to the empire of fashion'.[41] Fashion was not merely directing the 'choice of physicians, surgeons, apothecaries, and midwives'. Modern times showed something shockingly new: for fashion was nowadays directing the *beau monde* 'also in the choice of their diseases'.[42]

In short, the new aura of capitalist diseases was a hypochondriac's paradise of 'floating signifiers', disease names in frantic circulation unconstrained by authentic disease entities. And at the root of such fears was the dread of rampant imagination.

As crusty critics like Jonathan Swift leapt to insist, the entire new order was tainted by an epidemic of fancy. Newtonian science was grounded on a speculative metaphysics of invisible particles. The Walpolean economy was a house of cards built of paper money. And Locke's fashionable epistemology flagrantly denied the possibility of certain knowledge, deduced from clear and distinct ideas; all knowledge, Hume was soon to argue, was 'opinion'. How could this opportunity state ever be healthy if it were merely a pastiche of sensations and impressions? It is no accident that it was at this very time that the great modern disease of imagination, of wasteful spending – masturbation – began to haunt the public imagination, indexed by the runaway success of the medical scare-book, *Onania* (1710).[43]

Never were the links between mental dislocation and the economy of speculation more clearly and insistently elucidated than by Bernard Mandeville, the Rotterdam-born physician who perplexed his adopted country, England, with his paradoxes on this subject in the early years of the eighteenth century.[44] As a medical practitioner, Mandeville argued that he was living through times of fresh nervous disorders created by deceit and self-deceit, by the confusions of words and things, by speculation and imagination. His *Treatise of the Hypochondriack and Hysterick Diseases* (1730)[45] documented how surplus signs created sickness. In a fictitious dialogue conducted between a physician, Philopirio, a gentleman patient, Misomedon, and also his wife, Polytheca (their names immediately reveal their natures), Misomedon (who 'is very talkative' and 'seems to take Pleasure in talking of his Ailments') has, it is revealed, suffered a succession of excruciating maladies simply because, being affluent, leisured and educated, he read and imagined himself 'Hypochondriacus Confirmatus . . . a Crazy Valetudinarian'. He thereby gave himself, through the infections suggestiveness of medical symptoms, a chain of ailments which the mercenary medical profession had proved only too pleased to treat.[46] In short, Mandeville showed how an overripe imagination, adroit with signs, could be the cause of shocking illness: between them, Mandeville said, such patients and collusive doctors will reason 'a trifling Distemper into a Consumption', for words were diseases, and contagious ones at that.

Mandeville's dialogue bubbles with paradox. He shows Misomedon finally curing himself, of his self-inflicted hypochondria, merely by a form of the 'talking-cure' *avant la lettre*, pouring out his tale of woe to a wise physician. Personal reality was thus a closed system of signifiers, an echo chamber, without external referent. But that was equally Mandeville's perception of the socio-economic order, the realm of commercial capitalism. Capitalism was buoyed up by false appearances, by empty virtue and hypocrisy, as Mandeville unveiled in *The Grumbling Hive: or, Knaves Turn'd Honest* (1705), a moral tale, later decked out with lengthy prose commentaries and renamed *The Fable of the Bees: or Private Vices, Public Benefits* (1714).

Mandeville elucidated the conundrum of early capitalism. The nation was obviously availing itself of every opportunity to get on, get rich, accrue esteem and status. Yet enrichment was greeted with near-universal disapproval, a torrent of moral denunciation of gold, gain and greed. How so, then, and why? What was to be made of this? Was something to be done about it?

Interested, rather like Baudrillard, in legend and fantasies, Mandeville imaged a successful 'hive'. All the bees were ambitious egoists, striving to succeed by any possible means – by labour, trade, and other ways to earn an honest penny, but also rather shady and parasitical enterprises, such as the chicanery of the law, and unabashed swindles, frauds, roguery and theft on top:

> All trades and Places knew some Cheat,
> No calling was without Deceit.[47]

The conduct of the nation mirrored individual behaviour on a grand scale. It was, in other words, a proud, aggressive, warlike hive. Busy and bustling, both individuals and community flourished:

> Thus every Part was full of Vice,
> Yet the whole Mass a Paradise;
> Flatter'd in Peace, and fear'd in Wars,
> They were th'Esteem of Foreigners,
> And lavish of their Wealth and Lives,
> The Ballance of all other Hives.
> Such were the Blessings of that State;
> Their Crimes conspired to make 'em Great.[48]

What was the secret of the thriving hive? Vice:

> Thus Vice nursed Ingenuity,
> Which join'd with Time, and Industry
> Had carry'd Life's Conveniences

It's real Pleasures, Comforts, Ease,
To such a Height, the very Poor
Lived better than the Rich Before;
And Nothing could be added more.[49]

In short, a *trompe l'œil* economy of consumption flourished – that is, until Mortality intervened, and chose to crack the code. All was festering corruption, insisted the grumblers; the system fed on and rewarded vanity and greed. It fostered artificial desires that ran before strict needs. It was wanton and wasteful. Instead of disciplining, it vicariously excited the desires of the flesh. It produced luxury and debauchery. All this needed extirpation.

Rigorism had its way and day. Self-denial was inaugurated in the names of virtue and purity. Frugality became king, double-dealing ceased. The consequence? Dismal decline. Many trades began to disappear: no longer was there need for lawyers, or even doctors. Tailors and other dealers in frills and fripperies began to feel the pinch. Markets decayed, employment dropped off; recession was followed by a terminal slump. The Golden Age was restored, but at a price, for

In such Golden Times no body would dress above his Condition, no body pinch his family, cheat or overreach his Neighbour to purchase Finery, and consequently there would not be half the Consumption, nor a third part of the People employ'd as now there are.[50]

Rectitude and thrift had no need for a market economy. Hypocrisy, the inflation of signs, was at an end. If you wanted to bathe in righteousness, Mandeville concluded, you had to be prepared to feed off acorns.

Mandeville offered a choice. One could be poor and honest (i.e. operate a system of real needs, but without floating signifiers). Or one could engage in simulations, in Baudrillard's brothel of a world, initiating the symbolic exchanges which generated commercial exchanges. Over 250 years ago, I suggest, Mandeville was already arguing for the essential 'hysteria' of capitalism – a system fabricated upon façades or simulations, in a manner comparable to Baudrillard's account of the self-referential world of modern capitalism.

I say this, not to suggest that Mandeville, or anyone else, 'anticipated' Baudrillard. The point of my analysis is rather to insist that it is far too limiting an exercise to conceive of depicting the history of capitalism as a logic of rationality (that has maybe 'flipped' in recent times). Throughout its history, capitalist ideology has been utterly permeated with elements of fantasy, of the irrational and the imaginary, and stained with the implications of pathology and psychopathology.[51] I say this not to create any false expectation that capitalism will, by consequence, appear or prove more flimsy and fragile; but so that, when we seek to understand its tenacity, we will look in the right places. Of course Baudrillard and others are right, to some degree, to emphasize the revolutionary quality of the twentieth century, with its 'mass society' and 'mass media'. But these revolutions are also themselves integral to a secular evolutionary process – the multiplication of technologies, of literacies, of signs, of markets – that should be traced back at least as far as Gutenberg. Mass society, mass communications, the sign-saturated world have all been a long time coming.[52]

This point may be stated, by way of conclusion, somewhat more broadly. We have been deluged, over the last generation, by writings, both ecstatic and doom-laden, on 'postmodernity' (a phrase, incidentally, that Baudrillard was slow to take up).[53] We are endlessly being told that ours is an age in which, uniquely, everything is falling apart, imploding, suffering auto-critique, spinning out of the orbit of meaning, and so forth. 'Within postmodernism', Kuan-Hsing Chen has argued,

> our senses of the world, of the real, have largely been (re)defined by the explosion of mass media operation; media practices have rearranged our senses of space and time. What is real is no longer our direct contact with the world, but what we are given on the TV screen: TV *is* the world . . . History loses its referent, we enter into a new age of simulation.[54]

Clearly, the feeling is in the air. But the historian also requires to take all this with a large pinch of *déjà vu*.[55] *Mutatis mutandis*, all this could have been said – and was being said – of the age of Locke. And, after all, Nietzsche died, and *The Interpretation of Dreams* was published, in the nineteenth century. Yesterday's tomorrows suggest that we have often been there before. & so,

we can't wholly blame 'Simulacra, commodified
conscious, the Internet, speed-time
compression, pop music, etc for a (melancholy)
superficial sense of 'existence' – epistenology
& ontology. Ergo – back to the drawing board

NOTES

1 See Jean Baudrillard, *Le Système des objets*, Paris, Gallimard, 1968; *La Société de consommation*, Paris, Gallimard, 1970; *For a Critique of the Political Economy of the Sign*, St. Louis, Telos Press, 1981; *Le Miroir de la production*, Tournail, Casterman, 1973 (English translation *The Mirror of Production*, St. Louis, Telos Press, 1975). I made my first acquaintance with Baudrillard through the excellent collection of translations edited by Mark Poster: Jean Baudrillard, *Selected Writings*, Cambridge, Polity Press, 1989. I have found Poster's exegeses extremely helpful. I have also learned much from Mike Gane, *Baudrillard: Critical and Fatal Theory*, London, Routledge, 1991. Baudrillard owed much to Barthes. See Roland Barthes, *Mythologies*, trans. Annette Lavers, London, Cape, 1972; *Elements of Semiology*, trans. Annette Lavers and Colin Smith, London, Cape, 1967.

2 Originally a Marxist, from the time of writing *Le Miroir*, Baudrillard argued that Marxist economics and anthropology were but epicycles to bourgeois ideology. Marxism mirrored capitalism and hence needed to be broken into pieces.

3 Baudrillard, *Selected Writings*, p. 45 (from *La Société de consommation*). See also J. Baudrillard, *Simulacra and Simulations*, trans. Paul Foss, Paul Patton and Philip Beitchman, New York, Semiotext(e), 1983. Luminous on the evanescence of 'modernity' are Marshall Berman, *All that is Solid Melts into Air*, London, Verso, 1983; Steven Connor, *Postmodernist Culture: An Introduction to Theories of the Contemporary*, Oxford, Blackwell; John B. Thompson, *Ideology and Modern Culture*, Cambridge, Polity Press, 1990.

4 On the mysteries of hysteria, see Alan Krohn, 'Hysteria: the elusive neurosis', in *Psychological Issues*, 45/46, New York, International Universities Press, 1978. At the time of writing this essay (December 1991), the point was highlighted by the problematic relation between the vast carcase of the recently and mysteriously deceased capitalist swindler Robert Maxwell and the doomed body of his business empire, more illusion than reality.

5 On the analogues of the market, see J.-C. Agnew, *Worlds Apart: The Market and the Theater in Anglo-American Thought, 1550–1750*, Cambridge, Cambridge University Press, 1986.

6 W. Letwin, *The Origins of Scientific Economics*, London, Methuen, 1963; J. A. Schumpeter, *History of Economic Analysis*, London, Allen and Unwin, 1954; Hiram Caton, *The Politics of Progress: The Origins and Development of the Commercial Republic, 1600–1835*, Gainesville, University of Florida Press, 1988; David S. Landes, *The Unbound Prometheus: Technological Change and Industrial Development in Western Europe from 1750 to the Present*, London, Cambridge University Press, 1969.

7 Of course, Foucault is relevant here. See M. Foucault, *The Order of Things: An Archaeology of the Human Sciences*, Chs. 1 and 2, London, Tavistock, 1970; London, Routledge, 1989.

8 A. Marcovich, 'Concerning the continuity between the image of society

and the image of the human body: An examination of the work of the English physician J. C. Lettsom (1746–1815)', in P. Wright and A. Treacher (eds), *The Problem of Medical Knowledge*, Edinburgh, Edinburgh University Press, 1982, pp. 69–87.

9 A. Rabinbach, 'The body without fatigue: a nineteenth-century utopia', in S. Drescher, D. Sabean and A. Sharlin (eds), *Political Symbolism in Modern Europe: Essays in Honor of George L. Mosse*, London, Transaction Books, 1982, pp. 46–62; and his 'The European science of work: the economy of the body at the end of the nineteenth century', in Steven L. Kaplan and C. J. Koepp (eds), *Work in France: Representations, Meaning, Organization and Practice*, Ithaca, Cornell University Press, 1986, pp. 415–51; Norton Wise, with Crosbie Smith, 'Work and waste: political economy and natural philosophy in nineteenth-century Britain', *History of Science*, XXVII (1989), 263–301, 391–449; XXVIII (1990), 221–61.

10 Mikulas Teich and Roy Porter (eds), *Fin de Siècle and its Legacy*, Cambridge, Cambridge University Press, 1990; J. E. Chamberlin and S. L. Gilman (eds), *Degeneration: The Dark Side of Progress*, New York, Columbia University Press, 1985; Patrick Brantlinger, *Bread and Circuses: Theories of Mass Culture as Social Decay*, Ithaca, Cornell University Press, 1983; Brantlinger (ed.), *Energy and Entropy*, Indiana, University of Indiana Press, 1989.

11 R. H. Williams, *Dream Worlds: Mass Consumption in Late Nineteenth Century France*, Berkeley, California University Press, 1982; Roland Marchand, *Advertising the American Dream: Making Way for Modernity, 1920–1940*, Berkeley, University of California Press, 1985.

12 For mass hysteria, see Ian Dowbiggin, *Inheriting Madness*, Los Angeles, University of California, 1991; Jan Goldstein, 'The hysteria diagnosis and the politics of anticlericalism in late nineteenth century France', *Journal of Modern History*, LIV, (1982), 209–39; Goldstein, *Console and Classify: The French Psychiatric Profession in the Nineteenth Century*, Cambridge, Cambridge University Press, 1987; Robert Nye, *The Origins of Crowd Psychology: Gustave LeBon and the Crisis of Mass Democracy in the Third Republic*, London, Sage, 1975; Gustave Le Bon, *The Crowd: A Study of the Popular Mind*, trans. from the French, London, 1986; Max Simon Nordau, *Degeneration*, trans. from 2nd edn of the German work, London, Heinemann, 1920.

13 Lawrence Birken, *Consuming Desire: Sexual Science and the Emergence of a Culture of Abundance, 1871–1914*, Ithaca/London, Cornell University Press, 1989. The point is well explicated in Baudrillard, *Seduction*, London, Macmillan, 1990. The denial of desire could only ever be provisional. Hence Freud's explanation, to his young, hysterical patient, Dora – one equally applicable to the client on the couch and to a woman being seduced (where lies the difference?) – that, though we can say 'no', there can be no such thing as an unconscious 'no': 'noes' are but word-deep. Deep down, we are just seething masses of 'I want'. Our desires betray our denials. C. Bernheimer and Clare Kahane (eds), *In Dora's Case: Freud, Hysteria and Feminism*, New York, Columbia University Press, 1985.

14 Francis Gosling, *Before Freud: Neurasthenia and the American Medical Community, 1870–1910*, Chicago, University of Illinois Press, 1987; Tom Lutz, *American Nervousness, 1903: An Anecdotal History*, Ithaca, Cornell University Press, 1991; Edward Shorter, *From Paralysis to Fatigue. A History of Psychosomatic Illness in the Modern Era*, New York, Free Press, 1991.

15 Jean Baudrillard, *Cool Memories*, trans. Chris Turner, London, Verso, 1990, p. 11. See also Jean Baudrillard, *America*, London, Verso, 1988.

16 See the analyses in Mike Gane, *Baudrillard: Critical and Fatal Theory*, pp. 8f; Mark Poster (ed.), Jean Baudrillard, *Selected Writings*, pp. 4f.

17 For society as a body, see W. J. Greenleaf, *Order, Empiricism and Politics: Two Traditions of English Political Thought, 1500–1700*, London, Oxford University Press, 1964; F. Barker, *The Tremulous Private Body*, London, Methuen, 1984.

18 On early modern economic theory, see Joyce Appleby, *Economic Thought in Seventeenth-Century England*, Princeton, Princeton University Press, 1978; Albert O. Hirschman, *The Passions and the Interests: Political Arguments for Capitalism before its Triumph*, Princeton, Princeton University Press, 1977.

19 René Dubos, *The White Plague*, New Brunswick, Rutgers University Press, 1987.

20 Thomas Beddoes, *Hygeia: or Essays Moral and Medical, on the Causes Affecting the Personal State of our Middling and Affluent Classes*, 3 vols, Bristol, J. Mills, 1908, vol. 1, essay ii, p. 52. On Beddoes, see more broadly Roy Porter, *Doctor of Society: Thomas Beddoes and the Sick Trade in Late Enlightenment England*, London, Routledge, 1991.

21 Beddoes, *Hygeia*, 1.iii.11.

22 For these views, see John Brewer and Roy Porter (eds), *Consumption and the World of Good*, London, Routledge, 1992.

23 Beddoes, *Hygeia*, 1.iii.6, 10.

24 Ibid., 1.iii.84.

25 Ibid., 3.x.77.

26 This felicitous phrase is in C. B. Macpherson, *The Political Theory of Possessive Individualism: Hobbes to Locke*, London, Oxford University Press, 1962.

27 Beddoes, *Hygeia*, 1.ii.72.

28 Thomas Trotter, *A View of the Nervous Temperament, A Practical Enquiry into the Increasing Prevalence, Prevention, and Treatment of those Diseases Commonly Called Nervous, Bilious, Stomach and Liver Complaints; Indigestion; Low Spirits; Gout etc.*, London, Longman, 1807, p. xv.

29 Trotter, *View of the Nervous Temperament*, pp. 70, 27, 48.

30 Catherine Gallagher, 'The body versus the social body in the works of Thomas Malthus and Henry Mayhew', in Catherine Gallagher and Thomas Laqueur (eds), *The Making of the Modern Body: Sexuality and Society in the Nineteenth Century*, Berkeley, University of California Press, 1987, pp. 83–106; T. R. Malthus, *Essay on Population*, London, Macmillan, 1966 (1st edn, 1798).

31 I. Veith, *Hysteria: The History of a Disease*, Chicago, University of

Chicago Press, 1965; T. Szasz, *The Myth of Mental Illness*, New York, Paladin, 1961.

32 Thomas Sydenham, *Works*, London, Sydenham Society, 1848, vol. II, 54, *Epistolary Dissertation*. On Sydenham see K. Dewhurst, *Dr Sydenham 1624–1689*, Berkeley, University of California Press, 1966.

33 Sydenham, *Works*, II, 54.

34 For fuller discussion see Roy Porter, 'The rage of party: a glorious revolution in English psychiatry', *Medical History*, XXVII (January, 1983), pp. 35–50; Christopher Fox, *Locke and the Scriblerians: Identity and Consciousness in Early Eighteenth Century England*, Berkeley and Los Angeles, University of California Press, 1988; J. Yolton, *John Locke and the Way of Ideas*, Oxford, Oxford University Press, 1956.

35 G. Cheyne, *The English Malady; or, A Treatise of Nervous Diseases*, London, G. Strahan, 1733, p. 66.

36 Ibid., pp. 174 and 49.

37 Ibid., Preface, pp. i–ii.

38 Ibid., p. 34.

39 J. McKittrick Adair, *Essays on Fashionable Disorders*, London, Bateman, 1790, p. 1.

40 Ibid., p. 2.

41 Ibid., p. 3.

42 Ibid., pp. 4, 53. For the empire of fashion, see Neil McKendrick, John Brewer and J. H. Plumb, *The Birth of a Consumer Society: The Commercialization of Eighteenth-Century England*, London, Europa, 1982.

43 A slightly hysterical but insightful account of Locke as an abuser of words is offered in C. G. Caffentzis, *Clipped Coins, Abused Words, and Civil Government. John Locke's Philosophy of Money*, New York, Autonomedia, 1989; see also Ernest Lee Tuveson, *The Imagination as a Means of Grace: Locke and the Aesthetics of Romanticism*, Berkeley, University of California Press, 1960. On self abuse, see *Onania; or, The Heinous Sin of Self-Pollution, and all its Frightful Consequences*, London, J. Isted, 1710; Peter Wagner, 'The veil of science and mortality: some pornographic aspects of the ONANIA', *British Journal for Eighteen Century Studies*, IV (1983), pp. 179–84.

44 For essential Dutch background to Mandeville, see Simon Schama, *The Embarrassment of Riches: An Interpretation of Dutch Culture in the Golden Age*, London, Fontana, 1988.

45 B. Mandeville, *A Treatise of the Hypochondriack and Hysterick Diseases*, 2nd edn, London, Tonson, 1730; reprinted by George Olms Verlag, Hildesheim, 1981.

46 Ibid., pp. xii–xiii, 49, 202–5, passim.

47 B. Mandeville, *The Fable of the Bees*, ed. P. Harth, Harmondsworth, Penguin, 1970, p. 64.

48 Ibid., p. 67.

49 Ibid., p. 69.

50 Ibid., p. 219.

51 To say this is merely to reassert the insight of the founding fathers of

sociology that an irrationality lay at the heart of capitalism which sociology was required to analyse: see Max Weber, *The Protestant Ethic and the Spirit of Capitalism*, London, Allen & Unwin, 1930; Thorstein Veblen, *The Theory of the Leisure Class*, New York, Macmillan, 1912.

52 Marshall McLuhan, *Understanding Media: The Extension of Man*, London, A.R.K., 1987; Walter J. Ong, *Interfaces of the Word: Studies in the Evolution of Consciousness and Culture*, Ithaca, Cornell University Press, 1979.

53 See, for example, Mike Featherstone, *Consumer Culture and Postmodernism*, London, Sage, 1991.

54 K.-H. Chen, 'Baudrillard's implosive postmodernism', *Theory, Culture and Society*, III (1987), pp. 71–88.

55 Hillel Schwartz, *Ends of the Centuries*, New York, Free Press, 1991.

Chapter 2

The sweet scent of decomposition

Zygmunt Bauman

In the absence of a thorough statistical count of word distribution in Baudrillard's voluminous and still fast-growing *œuvre*, the reader has to settle for impressions. But impressions are forceful, difficult to avoid – and they are reinforced by every new page of reading.

Forsaken state. Collapse. Destruction. Malefice. Malicious. Suicidal. Subsuicidal. Devouring. Vorcity. Defunct. Obscene. Delirium. Vertiginous. Giddiness. Dizziness. Seizure. Convulsion. Epileptic. Vaginal. *Mammaire*. Humours. *Secretions. Glandulaire. Cellulaire*. Monstrosity. Cancer, cancerous. Metastasis. Hallucination. Shimmering. Mucous. Ooze. Viscosity. Flesh. Obesity. Excess. Excrescence. Orgy. Liquidity. Flux. Dungheap. Scatology. Laxative. Excremental. Putrefaction. Dead matter. Dead language. Dead bodies. Grave. Death. Scent. Seductive scent. Scent of seduction.

True, this is but a random selection. And yet not entirely random. Some words linger longer, leave deeper grooves than others. Perhaps because they reappear with a grinding monotony which cancels the reader's distance and preempts critical view, let alone resistance. Perhaps because of the heaviness of the semantic load each of them carries. Most likely, however, because – much like the countless dots and paint splashes on an impressionist canvas – they create a world in which they may dissolve, an image in which they are no more visible, a universe of meaning in which their own, private meanings, having done their job, are no longer identifiable, merging into a universe of experience that cancels meanings it cannot, and wishes not, to absorb.

What these words leave in their wake, as they run through pages – page after page after page – with growing speed, are not so much their own legible footprints, as an opaque cloud of diffuse sensations and shifty feelings. Contrary to what their literal, skin-thin semantics would suggest, these words do not address the sense of vision. Indeed, when mistaken for signs of visual images, they baffle or infuriate – or both. This is because these words are out of place in the orderly, binary, logically processed world ruled by the either/or and *tertium non datur*. These words are at home in a non-digital, non-discrete universe of vague, sticky, languishing sensations: in a tactile, olfactory universe. If treated as a chart of the world construed of boundary lines and digital sounds, Baudrillard's vocabulary can easily be shown to be semiotically impotent. But this vocabulary guides (is meant to?) into another world, one of touching and sniffing. Into a world where nose and fingertips, not eyes and ears, are the message.

Some critics have mistaken Baudrillard's universe for an alternative sociology. This is an error; the universe Baudrillard's vocabulary sustains is set in a different domain of experience and as such does not communicate with the realm of sociologically processed perceptions; as a matter of fact it entails few perceptions fit for orthodox sociological processing and concepts ready to be absorbed into orthodox sociological disourse. One may say that the first is a Dionysian, the second an Apollonian universe; but even this familiar metaphor is but of limited assistance, since one would need first to grasp the world through Dionysus's 'raw', uncultivated senses and thoroughly forget one's Apollonian training, to become a native in the Baudrillardian alternative space, to immerse oneself naively in the flow of impressions and 'forget' the anthropologist's compulsion to translate the 'foreign' into the 'familiar', the 'extraordinary' into the 'normal', the *distorted* into the *regular*. Perhaps the best way to approach Baudrillard's universe is to think of it as of an arduous and resolute effort to imagine what the world would look like were such a 'return' (a *transportation* rather) possible.

If one wants to follow Baudrillard in his labours, one should try to 'disarm' oneself – to abandon oneself to the normally silenced whispers and outlawed allusions. One should let the words conjure up the sensations they have been meant to, and are best to evoke – and these are, let us repeat, *tactile* and *olfactory* sensations. One would not *gaze* then through these words onto the familiar, well structured, semantically undisturbing pictures of life 'as we know it'. But one would *feel* viscous and mucous and sticky and oozy surfaces, and one would inhale pungent or acid, putrid or balmy, musky or spicy odours. An ability, Baudrillard suggests, of prime importance and first-rate survival in that world of ours, where simulacra have replaced the objects, contours of things have been blurred beyond recognition, and shapes serve to con and mislead, rather than to inform and guide: 'Since the world drives to a delirious state of things, we must drive to a delirious point of view' (Baudrillard 1990a: 9). The well structured and orderly habitat, once complete with foolproof instructions on how to sift the real from the imaginary, has decomposed, or is in the process of advanced decomposition (ours is a world of 'metastatic disorder, of multiplication through contiguity, of cancerous proliferation which does not obey any more the genetic code of value', a 'secret order of catastrophe' (ibid.: 15, 74)). No more can you go by what you see; shapes swim, wash away, vanish ('it is useless to appeal to rationality of the system against its excrescence' (ibid.: 74)). As they disintegrate, however, they exude tactile and olfactory evidence of putrefaction. If you wish to follow Baudrillard, do not trust your eyes, trust your nose and your fingers.

ODOURS OF CHAOS, ODOURS OF DANGER

Was it an accident that modernity declared war on smells? Scents had no room in the shiny temple of perfect order modernity set out to erect. And no wonder, as scents are the most obstreperous, irregular, defiantly ungovernable of all impressions. They emerge all on their own, and by doing so they betray what one would rather keep secret: that not everything is under control and not all is ever likely to be. Odours do not respect borderlines and do not fear border guards; they travel freely between spaces which – if order is to be preserved – have to be kept strictly apart. They cannot remain unnoticed, however hard one tries; one cannot isolate oneself from their presence the way one isolates oneself from sights by closing eyes or decreeing that eyes should be kept closed. Smells share with Simmel's strangers the upsetting habit of coming unannounced, outstaying their welcome, arriving now and refusing to go away later. They never really, truly, irrevocably vanish; they may – with great effort – be subdued, but they are hardly ever completely extinguished; when stifled by other scents, they do not in fact go away – they only bide their time, in a shallow shelter just a few inches below the threshold of sense, and wait for their chance; one cannot forget for a moment that they are but *temporarily suppressed and may reappear at any time, unexpected, shouting of the futility of master's mastery with which return; and one can be pretty sure that they will* reappear, unless something is done, and done again and again, to prevent them. Henri Bergson pointed out that 'comic' is what should be controlled but is not. This is why smells ridicule pretence of mastery, make solemnity laughable, embarrass and put to shame.

There were enough reasons, then, for the scents to turn into the sinister Other of everything modernity stood for: of order, predictability, control and self-control. As Alain Corbin (1982) has documented in his definitive account of the complex relationship between historic adventures of the sense of smell and the convolutions of social imagery, smells were cast as the vestige of animality in the human; as the emblem of savagery that defeated the drill of civilization; as the vivid testimony, and surest and least mistakable of signs, of the limits of rational control – and, indeed, of socially administered order. Smells were treacherous; and they were really and truly embarrassing, as the nagging reminder of failure.

Smells were to be disciplined. That means, not allowed to appear on their own initiative, in places of their choice, in their native, raw form. *Naturalness* in smells, like in everything else, was another name for barbarity, since *artificiality* – the designer reality – had become the trademark of civilization. In the total war against smells, the battle to conquer bodily odours was among the most ferocious. The territory vacated by natural odours was to be colonized by the artificially produced, and therefore controllable and controlled, scents. This was one of those battles that never stop. Momentary lapse of vigilance was, after all, enough for the exiled odours to crawl back. Excommunication of bodily odours kept the civilized person constantly on alert; it made the protection of the precarious state of civilization into a lifelong duty – a vocation which is never to be fully satisfied with its accomplishment.

Throughout the modern era, extermination of odours was one of the paramount activities in the daily struggle for creation and recreation of order – both personal and global. It was the means of personal redemption from the state of nature and personal elevation to the civilized state. It was also the tool of social division, production of social inferiority and social domination. As Georges Vigarello found out, the advocates of clean (*cleaned!*), odourless air hammered on the close link between stench and *dirt* (dirt, as

Mary Douglas explained, is the thing 'out of place', a thing that
defies the visualized order of things). 'But the places and bodies of
the nobility and the bourgeoisie were excluded; the suspect places
were where the poor gathered, and the suspect bodies those still not
protected by linen. It was first and foremost the common people
who were at issue' (Vigarello 1988: 146). Inferiority stank; it was
the opaque bottom layers of society, mean streets emanating vague
danger, places not yet reached by the iron fist of policed order, that
were marked by an array of odours simultaneously warning off and
repelling. There was a malodour of poverty, stench of cultural
savagery, fetor of the foreign races. The indolent, the rascals, the
aliens were *stinkers*. 'The rank compound of villainous smell'
'offended nostrils' (Shakespeare) and alerted to social danger. It
commanded to keep distance – spatial and social; the separation
from the carriers of untamed odours was necessary to prevent con-
tamination.

Keeping distance was not an easy matter, though. Populations
mixed, immigrants invaded the cities, strangers flooded public
places. Worst of all, the odours of the alien and the riff-raff defied
distances. One could arrest and confine the undesirables, but not
the stench they exuded. Odours travelled further and faster than
their carriers were ever allowed; they crossed boundaries at ease
and seeped through the tightest of locks. Obtrusive presence of
uncontrolled scents was vexing and off-putting. Because of it,
islands of superior living felt like fortresses permanently under
siege. Evidently, civilizational achievement was precarious and
revocable; and so had to be protected day and night.

> Manuals dealing with health changed their titles. Hitherto they
> had been concentrated on the maintenance or conservation of
> health. They now became treatises or manuals of hygiene . . .
> Hygiene was no longer an adjective qualifying health . . . but the
> collection of practices and knowledge which helped to preserve it
> . . . Medicine, at the end of the eighteenth century, had entered
> politics.
>
> (Vigarello 1988: 168)

Towards the end of the nineteenth century, with spatial and social
mobility gathering force and the separating walls rumbling under
the pressure, Europe succumbed to the panic of *decadence* and
degeneration. No victory over nature seemed final; no perfume

could extinguish the deadly, pestilent fetor of raw, uncivilized, decaying, mortal flesh.

To be 'smelly' was a cause of acute shame and embarrassment. The shame was joined by fear. Shame and panic drew strength from each other; it was believed that 'men died in confined spaces, of obscure bodily exhalations; their breath carried the poison of corrupt matter. Between this breath and the stink of corruption, whether of rubbish or of dead flesh, every possible analogy was drawn' (Vigarello 1988: 144). The mixture of embarrassment and horror spilled over the objects charged with repelling odours. As we all learned from Elias, such objects were swept under the carpets, flushed down the toilet, banished to distant and walled off places which the civilized humans never visited if they could help it; if you could not put it out of mind, at least you would try to keep it out of sight. Blood, raw flesh, naked body, the body reeking of *nature*, redolent of the smells reminding of unprocessed reality – became forbidden views. The eye and the nose joined forces in the war they did not expect to win. At best, the eye hoped to escape the terrors the nose could not avoid.

A few decades have passed, and here comes Baudrillard's description of the 'Japanese vaginal cyclodrama':

> Prostitutes, their thighs open, sitting on the edge of a platform, Japanese workers in their shirt-sleeves (it is a popular spectacle), permitted to shove their noses up to their eyeballs within the woman's vagina in order to see, to see better – but what? . . . if they could do it, these guys would be swallowed up whole within the prostitute. An exaltation with death? Perhaps . . . But why stop with nudity, or the genitalia? . . . Who knows what profound pleasure is to be found in the visual dismemberment of mucous membranes and smooth muscles?
>
> (Baudrillard 1990b: 31–2)

The eye wants to see what once the nose tried hard not to sniff? No player of the Japanese vaginal cyclodrama seems to be repelled; none is terrified; none is ashamed either. Instead, there is a genuine curiosity, earnestness of bona fide explorers, a sense of serious intellectual achievement, and a lot of unabashed satisfaction. The same motives and feelings, one would say, which send the American and British crowds to crash box-offices to watch with bated breath the decomposing flesh and the slow, relentless 'animalization' of a human in *The Fly*, to savour the sight of dismembered human bodies in successive instalments of *Friday the 13th*, or to queue for the video copies of *The Texas Chainsaw Massacre*. Elias told us that we would grow less and less tolerant of the morbid sights and smells of unprocessed, uncultured, untamed nature. Most evidently we do not. The threshold of shame and fear, once unstoppably on the way down, has shot up again and, as every film producer and video-library keeper would admit, the sky seems to be the limit. Something must have happened to reverse the trend. But what?

MODERNITY'S BEST KEPT SECRET

Human mortality used to be modernity's best kept secret. Modernity declared war on all constraints nature dared to impose upon rational and moral humanity – and mortality was foremost among them. Modernity fought death tooth and nail. Never seriously hoping to win the war, it focused instead on the somewhat more realistic project of coming top in each successive battle. In modern times, the 'total fact' of mortality was dissembled into a collection of mortal diseases and organic afflictions. Death became an event with a cause – an event which would not happen if only the cause – each cause, one by one – could be removed. One could not abolish death, but one could conquer every single one of its causes. Concentration on fighting single causes could, conceivably, keep people happy – since it kept them busy: there was always something to do to push back the end a tiny bit, and so little time was left to think of the end itself. No one seriously believed in immortality – but no one, as Freud found out, truly – actively, positively – believed in one's own death either; or, rather, one had no time to spare to chew and masticate such a thought.

Of death itself, modernity proud of its promotion of human omnipotence (and cosmic loneliness) had nothing exciting to say. In the world that made instrumentality a synonym for reason, death was one event that was not a means to any end (unless it was, of course, the death of an-other that served my, or our, end). Death had *no reason*, death was *unreasonable*. Death was a slap in the face of the proud, humiliation of the ambitious. This is why it had to be censored from daily life. The sight of dead and dying was out of bounds – only trained experts were allowed to face it. As to the ordinary mortals – only tamed sights, carefully arranged, heavily varnished with human design, painted all over with the florid traces of human labour, were to surround them from now on (like all forbidden sights, death could burst into vision only in the form of pornography – as Gorer pointed out forty years ago). The reassuringly durable surface could, conceivably, hide the horrifyingly transient subsoil (even though the cover-up itself was evidently transient; unlike the incurable transience it hid, the cover-up could be in principle, started anew and repeated). 'A woman', remarks Baudrillard, 'may be so heavily made up that you can never be certain of her disappearance. Life can be so mystified that you can never be sure of its opposite' (1990c: 66). If properly made up, the smile does outlive the Cheshire cat. The products of processing must no longer go down with the raw stuff that has been processed: this was one of the most alluring among modernity's promises.

The promise has not been fulfilled, but it was precisely its unfulfilment that kept it alive and effective. There was so much to do before the day of reckoning could come – and it would not come as long as something to be done had not been done yet. 'Death sentence', says Baudrillard, 'generally stays cosily tucked away, hidden beneath the difficulty of living. If that difficulty is removed from time to time, death is suddenly there, unintelligibly' (1990c: 67). Paradoxically, the key to keeping the promise alive is to invent more fears (providing these are nice, little, manageable fears – ghosts that appear only together with foolproof recipes for exorcism), to make life busier, more difficult, until the whole life-space is filled with worries. Keeping dieting-abstaining-exercising is a full time job, one that leaves little room for anything else; the most thriving of modern industries, the production of risks and fears, would never allow the job to be less full. The characteristically modern way of defusing the perennial horror of mortality is to dissemble the intractable irreversibility of death into the infinite chain of all-too-human, practical, mundane tasks and worries. The leftovers – whatever privately administered tasks blatantly cannot handle – are removed beyond the realm of lay concerns and made invisible for the lay eye; they are put in the hands of the experts, shrouded in obstruse mystery of specialist language and skills.

Hiding the truth of mortality (its *irreversibility*, its resilient, all-culture-defying 'naturalness', its immunity to *all* cultural manipulation) was the *conditio sine qua non* of the success of this strategy of deconstruction. What needed to be hidden in the first place was the evidence that all human beautification of the mortal body is, literally, no more than skin deep (from time to time we are frightened by the sight of the 'interior of the smoker's lung' or the 'interior of the drinker's stomach'. Are not, however, all lung or stomach interiors frightening, in their lofty disregard for our power to control and manipulate, in their obtuse, deadly immunity to our health-and-fitness bustle?). More closely guarded than anything else had to be the secret of the body's relentless decomposition, oblivious to all efforts, however solemnly certified was their guarantee of success.

Keeping away the odours of decomposition (and all natural bodily odours are odours of decomposition, as they cannot but remind of the fickleness of all promises to the contrary), as well as the sights that arouse memory of such odours, was indispensable – if the modern expedient of deconstruction were to work and mortality were to be effectively banned from the life-world. But what if, for a change, transience itself becomes the acknowledged norm of life? If not mortality, but *immortality* is deconstructed?

The terror of death may be exorcized in more than one way. Yet, however varied and numerous, all ingenious techniques of exorcism may be roughly divided into two basic classes. One follows the principle 'we'll cross that bridge once we come to it'; it admits that the bridge will have to be crossed sometime, but insists that the time of the crossing may be postponed – perhaps indefinitely (the current craze of *cryonics* represents this hope at its radical *privatized* extreme; immortality of the nation or other 'causes' has long offered the extreme collectivized version). The second – one that seems to be favoured by the world we live in – makes the whole of life into a game of bridge-crossing, so that all bridges seem alike, all are comfortably part of a daily itinerary, and no bridge seems to loom ominously as the 'ultimate' one. Crossing the bridge becomes a habitual, sometimes even pleasurable activity – all the more so for the fact that each crossing practised thus far has been *reversible*. None of the bridges has been a one-way road. Like odours, all objects seem to linger around forever, even if for a time they stay invisible. Nothing vanishes for good. There is no 'point of no return' – nothing that has been botched cannot be done better next time. No loss is irretrievable.

This new experience has been captured well by Guy Debord:

> Media/police rumours acquire instantly – or at worst after three or four repetitions – the indisputable status of age-old historical evidence. By the legendary authority of the spectacle of the day,

odd characters eliminated in silence can reappear as fictive survivors, whose return can always be conjured up or computed, and *proved* by the mere say-so of specialists. They exist somewhere between the Acheron and the Lethe, these dead whom the spectacle has not properly buried, supposedly slumbering while awaiting the summons which will awake them all . . .

(Debord 1990: 55)

It is immortality itself that now becomes mortal. But the sting of finality has been pulled out from mortality, all mortality, including the mortality of immortality: mortality is but a suspension, a transitional state. A suspension that is itself 'immortal' – permanent, assured to last forever (all is securely stored on computer disks, anyway). 'When the spectacle stops talking about something for three days, it is as if it did not exist. For it has gone on to talk about something else, and it is that which henceforth, in short, exists' (1990: 20). Do not worry, though:

The manufacture of the present where fashion itself, from clothes to music, has come to a halt, which wants to forget the past and no longer seems to believe in future, is achieved by the ceaseless circularity of information, always returning to the same short list of trivialities.

(Debord 1990: 13)

Objects come and go, but then come again, never to overstay their visit. They are condemned to the nomadic existence of commerical travellers. Last year's rubbish becomes the cherished antique, the last generation's fallen star turns into the idol of nostalgic dream, the killing fields of yore are invaded by pilgrims searching for 'our glorious heritage' of industrial or military triumphs. What was obsolete yesterday becomes a rage of today, and is doomed to slip once more into oblivion even before it has forced its way, with a fanfare, into the centre of today's attention. Mortality daily rehearsed turns into immortality; everything becomes immortal, and nothing is. Only transience is durable.

Have not the objects become more like odours, that never go away for good, that are only temporarily crowded away by other scents, only to reappear triumphantly again, and again, and again? Truth of such a reality is to be *inhaled* rather than scanned. Or, rather, the vision itself turns olfactory.

IMMORTALITY'S VANISHING ACT

> What has disappeared has every chance of reappearing. For
> what dies is annihilated in linear time, but what disappears
> passes into the state of constellation. It becomes an event in a
> cycle which may bring it back many times.
>
> (Baudrillard 1990c: 92)

> Nothing disappears any more through an end or death, but
> through proliferation, continuity, saturation and transparence
> . . . No more *mode fatal* of disappearance, only *mode fractal* of
> dispersion.
>
> (Baudrillard 1990a: 12)

Death and disappearance are two sharply distinct modes of 'ceasing
to be'. As sharply distinct are the worlds in which one or the other
gains prevalence. Let us call them, for the sake of convenience,
A-world and B-world respectively.

A-world is a *succession* of beings. It is a world of *finality* – of
scarcity of space. Space is at a premium. Beings must vacate the
place they occupy if other beings are to appear. Thus beings have
their *beginnings* – they are born (that is, they were not in the world
before, but they are now), and they have their *ends* – they die (that
is, they are in the world now, but they will not be). Of these two
events in the biography of beings the first is reversible (revocable):
a being which is here today may not be tomorrow. The second is
irreversible (irrevocable): a being that ceased to be will not be
again. It is only of the second event that one can say that it is
'final', 'forever'. No birth contains promise of durability, permanence, *immortality*. Only death does – and its promise of
immortality carries the weight of certainty.

B-world, on the other hand, is a *coexistence* of beings. It is a
world in which space is not scarce. Or, rather, space has many
levels, its living floors and its cellars, open stages and hidden
limbos. To make room at one level, beings may, and do, just move
to another. True, beings are born (though they try to hide it, presenting themselves as quotations, past remembered, tradition
restored); but once born, they stay – it is the event of birth, distant
or recent, that is now irrevocable and irreversible. True, beings still
undergo transformations *superficially* similar to death; indeed,
they vanish from sight and cease to communicate. Yet the resemblance to death is but superficial, since unlike death their departure

is reversible and revocable; one can always 'recover' the vanished beings from the limbo where they reside (reversibility, says Baudrillard – 'cyclical reversal, annulment', 'puts an end to the linear time' [1988a: 120]. Linear time is, as a matter of fact, a metaphor, or a visual representation, for the idea of 'no return'). Unlike death, disappearance is not final, not 'forever'; there is no certainty of its permanence.

In the B-World immortality is, so to speak, a birth right. By the same token, it has none of the attractions that surround it in the A-World. It is not a challenge to be taken up, a task to be performed, a reward to be earned. Neither is it a project that can give meaning to the being-in-the-world. In the B-World, immortality dissolves in the melancholy of presence, in the monotony of endless repetition.

In the B-World, both life and death lose their colours. Disarmed death (now transformed into a dull, lingering, limbo-like existence – a confinement without a sentence specifying its duration) remakes life into its own likeness. It is as if life originally meant for a finite life-span yet now spread, beyond its capacity, over eternity, does not suffice to keep the balloon of life inflated, and leaves behind but a limp and flaccid shroud. Samuel Beckett's *End* is a story about meaninglessness of being that does not end. It starts with the event of a funeral, but in a truly B-World style death and burial are not the end of being, but mere disappearance. The state of disappearance is not strikingly different from life; by the same token, life loses much of what, allegedly, set it apart from non-life. 'Strictly speaking I wasn't there. Strictly speaking I believe I've never been anywhere.' Thus, looking back, into what was thought to be different but was not, 'the memory came faint and cold of the story I might have told, a story in the likeness of my life, I mean without the courage to end or the strength to go on'.

Only finite objects, only irreversible events have the obstreperous solidity which we call 'reality'. They are serious and command respect. One may, perhaps, ward them off or delay; once they occur, however, they cannot be undone. Because events are irreversible, 'unanticipated consequences' turn into the most sinister of nightmares, 'the unpredicted' becomes the most ignoble failure, and 'the uncontrolled' appears to be the most unnerving of challenges. Irreversibility thus favours foresight, examination, calculation, planning. It enthrones the faculty of reason, trusted to possess all those skills, in the managing seat.

Reason becomes the being's principal weapon in the A-World, where it is death, the permanent cessation of being, which is irreversible; where irreversibility stands against being, threatening its continuance. Reason, though, may well lose its central place in the B-World, where being itself is irreversible, and thereby unthreatened. With death replaced by disappearance, disempowered, denied irreversibility – the weapon of reason becomes superflous. And so become gratuitous the prime functions of reason – differentiation and choice. With these functions redundant, the two arms of reason fall into disuse – 'the faculty to conceive of something and the faculty to "represent" something' (Lyotard 1991: 25). (With those two arms, reason used to produce reality. Reason is about the separation of the real from the apparent – the 'truly real' from 'pseudo-real', the real that is, really, what it claims to be, from the deceitful pretence of reality. Reason determines the reality which is its domain, like the producers determine their products. The 'irreal', by the same token, stands for everything which reason does not control. Reason is, and must be, relentlessly vigilant against *trompe l'œil*, that devil's cauldron where all the monsters of contingency, unpredictability and uncontrollability are cooked up.) What falls into disuse, moreover, is the very distinction between the two facilities. Conception dissolves in representation; representation *is* conception. Being lives in being represented, and it does not have any other life to live.

In the A-World, beings cannot be taken at face value, and not taking them at face value is, literally, a matter of life and death. It is *vital* to know what they *in fact* are, since being different from what they seem to be may be *fatal*. Beings are suspected of hiding as much, if not more, as they are trusted with revealing. Hence the imperative of lie detectors, of truth testing, of obsessive search for proofs and certificates of sincerity. Beings are just *signifiers* – appearances floating on the surface of solid reality. They may not be always deceitful, but they are always opaque. It takes an effort to pierce their opacity, to 'see through them' into that reality which cannot be changed – though its representations, signifiers, appearances, can and do. The A-World cannot but be obsessed with *interpretation*. Things are to be tested for the degree of dissimulation. The testing never stops. One needs 'to get the facts straight' – to 'get down to the real thing' prostrated in the shadow of its sign. But the road never seems to end – there is another depth beneath the one already reached. What the signifier points to, proves to be, at a closer look, just another signifier.

In the B-world, on the other hand, there is no existence solid or soft, durable or elusive, more and less trustworthy. Everything that is, is for good; forever. What is seen and heard need not therefore be mistrusted. The modality of talking is not inferior to the modality of that which is being talked about. Representation which is not a derivative, subordinate version of what is being represented, is no more a representation (not a 'mere representation'): it need not be held under surveillance, put under the microscope as, possibly, 'mere appearance'. All beings beckon to each other, are beckoned back, there are loops instead of straight lines, exploration of each route returns ultimately to the starting point. After a number of detours, the signifiers fall upon themselves.

One may legitimately suspect *dissimulation* in any act of *simulation*; but in the B-World beings *do not* simulate any more. Simulation, like dissimulation, connotes feigning and deception; deception, in its turn, invokes the presence of the 'real things' which can be feigned, misrepresented (suspicion of fraud is an oblique tribute to the invincibility of truth). The worry about simulation is born, in other words, of a strict distinction between the signifiers and what they signify. But there is no such distinction if signification does not discriminate and thus does not degrade, if beings signify but each other in a closed circle, if signification is mutual, if all objects have the same solidity, or suffer the same dearth of solidity, if they are all engaged in the same never-ending cadrille of disappearances and reappearances.

The A-World is preoccupied with the search for meaning. Meaning is, after all, the relation between elusive appearance and solid, yet hidden, reality. Meaning is the hard, yet invisible core wrapped tightly in what offers itself to the senses, what can be seen and heard: the signifier. That core can be recovered if the carapace of the signifier is broken. The A-World needs detectives; Sherlock Holmes, who never trusted things to be what they seemed, is that world's archetypal hero. Yet the detective true to his name never treats things lightly – however untrustworthy he suspects them to be. They may bear false evidence, but they are *evidence* all the same. Appearances lie; but to say that they lie is to corroborate (indeed, to construe) the existence of truth. Mistrust of appearances sustains (and is sustained by) the unshakeable trust in 'real things'. However misleading, the appearances are charged with *meanings*.

The B-World, on the other hand, has no time for Sherlock Holmes. Not that the B-World agrees to live at peace with a lie (whenever alerted to a lie, the residents of that world would be pushed off course and react angrily and neurotically); but having been awarded immortality at birth, all things stand ultimately for nothing but themselves – there is no division between things that mean and things that are meant. More exactly, each such division is but momentary, protean, and ultimately reversible. 'There is nothing outside the text' (Derrida); there is no 'outside' in the game of signs. It is just by linguistic inertia that we still talk of signifiers bereaved of signifieds, as signifiers; of signs which stand but for themselves, as 'appearances'.

'Only signs without referents, empty, senseless, absurd and elliptical signs, absorb us . . . The mind is irresistibly attracted to a place devoid of meaning.' It is 'non-sense that seduces'; seduction employs 'signs without credibility and gestures without referents' (Baudrillard 1990b: 74–5). The theorists of A-World would tell us that the hide-and-seek play of appearances and reality is the domain of *episteme*; on their own, appearances stay in the inferior domain of *doxa* – 'mere beliefs'. In B-World, beliefs do not supplant knowledge; it is rather that *seduction* renders meaningless the very distinction between beliefs and knowledge, theorized as a divide between appearances and reality. Seduction cancels the division. That which seduces is not an appearance – and its power of seduction derives from its immunity to the sort of interrogation which one would address to an appearance. It is after all the *semantic void* that seduces. Seduction is like the 'sucking power' of a whirlpool; better still, like that force which moves the jet engine: 'the jet engine is no longer an energy of space-penetration, but propels itself by creating a vacuum in front of it that sucks it forward . . . movement produces the vacuum that sucks you in' (Baudrillard 1988b: 11). Such a world that has been emptied of meaning, that abolished the very referentiality of the sign and de-legitimized the questions about reality *behind* the appearances, is – in Baudrillard's vocabulary – a *hyperreality*.

Like any vacuum, and because it is a semantic vacuum, hyper-reality 'sucks in' – *seduces*. Unlike the hold of reality (which can be uncovered only if appearances have been swept away – and therefore carries forever a mark of the broom), the force of hyperreality is unconditional and its power is absolute; that power works through fascination. One walks into the trap as if in a trance, bewitched, not really in control of one's steps: there is nothing to warn one off and bring back the critical sense out of its swoon.

Perhaps an image of a bumble-bee lured by the gluey and syrupy aroma of flowers will capture that form of life which words, geared to the analytical faculties of reason, can represent only as sickly anomaly. This is, after all, a form of life of which those analytical faculties can only conceive as of orgiastic ecstasy, a 'self-losing of the individual'. This is, as Michael Maffesoli suggested, a form of life of the theatre, and in the theatre each scene – serious, not very serious, and not at all serious – counts: 'in theatricality nothing is important, because everything is important' (Maffesoli 1985: 16–18).

A-World, Baudrillard would say, is ruled by *law*; B-World is guided by the *rule*. Law prescribes, inhibits and prohibits. By the same token, it creates the possibility of transgression or its own abolition; it draws a benchmark for *liberation*, as well as for conspiracy, clandestinity, hidden transcripts and latent discourse. None of these is done by the rule. Rule is not a set of constraints imposed on the world: rule is the whale on which the world rests. Take it away, and the world shall capsize and vanish. 'It makes no sense to "transgress" a game's rules; within a cycle's recurrence, there is no line one can jump (instead, one simply leaves the game)' (1990b: 132). If all players leave, the game ceases to be (rules 'exist only when shared, while the Law floats above scattered individuals' (p. 136)). But in B-World many games go on at the same time, and each player has a wide choice of rules. If each set of rules conjures up and sustains its own game, its own mini-world, one can enter and leave worlds at will, each stay being solely 'until further notice'. One thing the player cannot do is opt out from playing altogether. There is no other world but many rule-guided games; no tough, resilient, stubborn world held in place by legal repression. Each game has (an)other game(s) for a neighbour – but together, the games leave nothing outside. They have no 'exteriority' still waiting to be invaded and colonized. No game aspires to universality, and 'there is no metaphysics looming on the horizon of the game's indefinitely reversible cycle (p. 147). Games are cyclical and recurrent; they 'reproduce a given arbitrary constellation in the same terms an indefinite number of times' (p. 146). Games promise *eternal return*. Doing so, they deliver the players 'from the linearity of time and death' (p. 146). Once more, everything is immortal, and so nothing is; nothing is *privileged* by its durability in the world that cancelled the distinction between the durability of the game and the transience of every move.

Game (and thus B-World as a whole) is not a realm of chance, distinct from the orderly and determined sequences of the law-ruled A-World. The very notion of chance makes sense only within the law-guided world of determination, and B-World is not such a world. Chance is the abominable Other of the world of law. Put the rule in place of law, and the chance vanishes together with the norm in which it dwelled as its not-yet-fully-exorcized 'inner demon'. Games deny objective determination, but they deny also objective *contingency*: 'the basic assumption behind the game is that chance does not exist', 'that the world is built of networks of symbolic relations – not contingent connections, but webs of obligation, webs of seduction. One has only to play one's hand right . . .' (pp. 143–4).

No determination, no chance; just a soft, pliable game without set or predictable denouement that exhausts itself fully in the aggregate of players and their moves. The player cannot determine the outcome; nor are the player's moves devoid of consequence. As there is no law that links action to its outcome, there is no clear prescription what one should do in order to attain the result one wishes. This world offers no certainty – but no despair either; only the joy of a right move and the grief of a failed one.

CIVILIZATION MINUS DISCONTENTS

Sometimes explicitly, sometimes obliquely, Baudrillard hammers home a message which, in the terms that have been developed above, could be expressed in the following propositions:

– We live now, by and large, in B-World.
– This B-World in which we live is a product of the decomposition of A-World.
– B-World includes the awareness that it is a product of such decomposition.
– That awareness disarms all self-critique, as it is precisely the right to be critical that has been decomposed.

Decomposition; but a strange one. Not the decomposition we normally think of when we hear the word. To repeat after Lyotard, the A-World of modernity has not been abandoned; it remains very much with us and around us – perhaps never more than now, in its posthumous life. It is not dead: it *disappeared*, dissolved in the ostensible completion of its task. This eerie decomposition is, in

Baudrillard's words, *pathology of the third type* – product not of a disease, of the *ab*normal, but of *a*nomaly which has turned into the norm. 'In a world cleansed of past infections, in a clinically "ideal" world, spreads an impalpable, implacable pathology, born of disinfection itself' (1990a: 69). The modern project did not fail. Its undoing was its success – too overwhelming, too complete. The quest for order has produced a hygroscopic, sanitized, hygienic bubble – odourless and germless; the inside of the bubble has lost immunity, capacity to be alerted by incoming danger, to defend itself: to tell danger from happiness, evil from the norm. The decomposition is, accordingly, odourless and sanitized; our olfactory faculties of self-defence have been long put to sleep by the thick cloud of deodorizing perfume. The danger is now without odour.

Our world hides the secret of decomposition beneath its glittering surface, and decomposition is there because the inner energy of the emancipation drive, needed to keep the bubble inflated and impregnable, is all gone. The inner rot shows itself on occasion, in the sheer spectacularity of world-wide catastrophes: AIDS, for instance, is a product of the disarmed defences turning against the very organism they were supposed to defend (1990a: 71). This kind of decomposition is the liminal state of the anti-decomposition drive. This heart of darkness is on the far side of light. The bankruptcy of the modern order, if there is one, has been caused by its own excesses: by the heaps of waste which the obsession with order could not but spawn, and thus by the unbearable, prohibitive cost of waste disposals. In a world in which (revocable) disappearance replaced (irrevocable) death, nothing dies, nothing disappears for good; no waste can be disposed of radically and completely, it can only be recycled – and recycling of waste is in itself a waste-producing process. The outcome is a swollen, obese existence, in which health and disease change places and lose meaning: there is 'continuation of all categories', tantamount to the 'substitution of one sphere for another, confusion of genres'; 'each category is pushed to a too large degree of generalization, losing all its specifity, dissolving in all the others' (1990a: 16–17).

The dangers the world faces on the other side of modernity are all of its own making. To stand up to such dangers, it would need to cast a critical eye upon itself. There is little point in searching for enemies outside or the fifth column inside. For a world that is threatened by its own decomposition, *self*-critique is the only salvation. But does self-critique have a chance?

The B-World of postmodernity is not actively, programmatically, wilfully, consciously, anti-critical; it is not conservative in the sense of ideological commitment to preservation or restoration. It is rather that the occasion to be critical about the foundations of that world does not arise – not inside of it quotidianity, at any rate; and this is, primarily, because the distinction between foundation and the 'merely present' has been all but erased. In this world, simulation is the principal procedure through which reality is made up, while it pretends to be merely 're-constructed' or 're-presented'.

Simulation is no longer that of a territory, a referential being or a substance. It is the generation by models of a real without origin or reality; a hyperreal. The territory no longer precedes the map, nor survives it. Henceforth, it is the map that precedes the territory – *precession of simulacra* – it is the map that engenders the territory and if we were to revive the fable today, it would be the territory whose shreds are slowly rotting across the map. It is the real, and not the map, whose vestiges subsist here and there, in the deserts which are no longer those of the Empire, but our own. *The desert of the real itself.*

(Baudrillard 1988a: 166)

Simulation is not a lie (to perceive it as a lie, one must first tacitly assume that 'the territory precedes the map' – accept the claim that reality exists separately from and independently of simulation). Nor is the simulation a contraption to hide the absence of reality (this purpose is served by casting certain simulations as *dis*simulations – fakes, cover-ups, misinformations – suggesting by the same token that there is something really genuine, which can be covered up or *mis*represented). B-World-type simulation is, to enter the spirit of Baudrillard's phraseology, 'more simulated than simulation' – a *hypersimulation*, so to speak: 'it bears no relation to any reality whatsoever: it is its own pure simulacrum' (1988a: 170). Or, to paraphrase Derrida, one could say: *il n'y a pas dehors de simulacre.*

It is easy to see that A-World was, and could not but be, self-critical. One can say that discontent with itself is the most decisive of its traits. As Lyotard recently explained, this has been so because the A-World in its modern incarnation was held together and set in motion by a peculiar (and in historical terms idiosyncratic) legitimizing myth: not a myth of a discriminating and tribalizing 'foundational act', a past act, irreversible and permanently definitional –

but of an idea (of freedom, of wisdom, of justice, of equality, or whatever) which is universal but whose universality lies in the future, still waits to be accomplished, *demands* to be accomplished. Such a legitimating myth denies the present its authority; it down-grades the present to the status of an imperfect, immature form of the future, a transient and contingent state whose only value is in the speed in which it transforms itself. Modernity could not think of itself, comprehend itself, get hold of itself intellectually, without distancing itself critically from any of its historically achieved implementations. This is how Lyotard unpacks Habermas's concept of modernity as a 'project'. 'My argument' – says Lyotard – 'is that the modern project (of realizing universality) has not been abandoned or forgotten, but destroyed, "liquidated" ' (1991: 36). I suggest that what has been 'liquidated', or rather decomposed, is precisely the characteristically modern mode of 'deconstruction of mortality' guided by the thrust to immortal perfection, and conse-quently of the modern mode of delegitimizing the present as no more than a local and transient obstacle to universal and durable accomplishment.

B-World, in its postmodern incarnation, has no reason to cavil or be dismissive about its present. More precisely, it has no *legitimation* for such a stance; no legitimizing myth that would lend confidence to the critics of its practices and put the critics of criticism on the defensive. This trait has often been misinterpreted as the postmodern world's satisfaction with itself; or, obversely, as putting an end to the notorious propensity of modern civilization to spawn discontent (through a somewhat convoluted logic, such mis-interpretation allowed Habermas and his followers to insist that a mere recognition of the contemporary condition as 'postmodern' is tantamount to assuming an uncritical, even laudatory, stance toward that condition; that, therefore, the analysts who define the present condition as postmodern are immanently, or even self-consciously, conservatives). No great effort is needed to see that the conclusions stem from the premise which the de-composition of the modern project has disallowed: namely, that the legitimizing authority of all discourse rests solely in the idea which may claim universality. (This premise, let us observe, was from the start tainted with the error of *petitio principi*: the present had been decried as 'mere appearance' because it was not up to the standard of universality, but it was the pet image of universality that made it appear substandard in the first place.) Whoever denies that premise, allegedly rejects the very possibility of critique; indeed, critique that lacks authoritative legitimation does not deserve the name, and certainly cannot (would not?) be treated seriously nor hope to leave a trace on the world's practice.[1]

It cannot be denied that the postmodern condition may give an excuse to those who desire to get rid once and for all of the disquieting and notoriously uncomfortable idea that the world as it is is not the best of possible worlds and that one could improve on its present state. That is, it may give an excuse – if one needed one. The point is, however, that people who preach getting rid of the above-mentioned idea with the strongest zeal and gusto do not need an excuse, do not seek excuse; and if they did, they most certainly would not look for it in the transformation of the world 'out there' (or in any historically or socially constituted reality, for that matter). The 'postmodernist philosophers', who – exactly like Habermas, though without his grief or despair – insist that one can be 'critical' only with one's feet firmly set on the rock of absolute and universal truth, would be the last to accredit their own programmatically uncritical stance to the stage of history, form of society and other mundane transformations; they would be the last to legitimize their 'emancipation from emancipation' in terms of the form their society has taken. Postmodern philosophers neither have nor need the concept of postmodernity. They would certainly prefer it not to be around – lest their sudden discovery of the original error besetting the 'Cartesian–Lockean–Kantian paradigm' should smack of an historically and socially determined event, rather than a free choice of free-roaming and self-determining thought.

But Baudrillard's description of postmodernity is sustained by a sociological, not a philosophical discourse. In Baudrillard's story, postmodernity emerges as a product of decomposition of a certain historically shaped form of life called modernity; as the end result of that form of life implementing itself in full and arriving at its own 'unanticipated consequence', where – a victim of its own success – it is being transformed into its own negation. In this vision, critique is not cast as an *error*, as in the postmodern philosophical discourse; instead, it is the historically determined *difficulty* of critique that is explored and portrayed; a difficulty in the socio-cultural, practical sense – not in the sense of logical inelegance or downright incongruence of the critique's legitimation (it is the latter – philosophical, not Baudrillardian – sense, that stems ultimately from taking postmodern *simulacra* at their face value).

What makes of the postmodern setting an environment inhospitable to critique, is not the discovery of the philosophical illegitimacy of the critical stance, but the numerous and powerful obstacles against dissidence built into the structure of the lifeworld; or, more precisely, the many factors militating against the build-up of disaffection into a forceful anti-systemic dissidence.

Such factors are indeed many, but they boil down in the end to the decomposition of structured, 'hard' reality into the play of simulacra, in which simulation and dissimulation merge, in which a deeper reality is implied where it is all displayed at the surface, while genuine necessities without choice hide under the mask of free game ('We live in the mode of *referendum* and this is precisely because there are no more referentials.' But 'referendum is really just an ultimatum . . . Each message is a verdict [1988a: 142]). Boundless dependency hides beneath the ploy of freedom; it does not coerce, it seduces – through the pretended weakness, malleability, unreadiness of the world. Perhaps the most insidious of simulacra, a true meta-simulacrum, is the constraint dressed as free choice. The postmodern world seduces its residents by its alleged emptiness, implied absence of a second line of trenches, putative lack of resistance. It offers itself as the realm of freedom achieved, emancipation accomplished – and thus energy is sucked off all prospective emancipatory projects. Liberty is here and now. 'If one needed to characterize the present state of affairs, I would say this is a situation after the orgy. That orgy, is the explosive movement of modernity, one of the liberation in all realms.' 'All finalities of liberation are already behind us . . . We accelerate in a void' (1990a: 4). Let us inhale the sweet incense of decomposition of everything that has been once tough, harsh, inflexible and resilient; let us immerse ourselves in the exhilerating joys of the free-for-all game called life. Let us? There is pretty little we could do otherwise. Nothing is left to fight for; there is nothing one can demand that the world cannot deliver (as the world has seen to it that nothing is demanded except what it can, and wants to, deliver).

In the world which makes freedom into necessity (having first made necessity feel like freedom) disaffection is aplenty. The price of survival is still, as before, the agony of frustration and the horror of failure. If in the oppressive modern world of naked necessities, however, agony and horror blended into projects of collective emancipation, in the seductive postmodern world of ostentatious liberty they stay apart in a loose heap of non-additive personal tragedies. One does not blame the rules for losing a game. The remedy for a defeat in the game lost yesterday is to win the game played today or tomorrow. Losers have no less reason than the winners to wish that the game goes on, and that its rules stay in force; and no more reason to want the game to be proscribed or its rules overhauled. Postmodernity enlists its own discontents as its most dedicated storm-troopers. At no other time has dissent resided so dangerously close to collaboration.

This is, to use Elias's terms, the *figuration* which sets today the limits of possible strategies and divides the latter into 'realistic' and 'misconceived'. Blaming Baudrillard for the narrowness of the limits is no more up to the point than the proverbial condemnation of the messenger for the bad news he brings. Emancipatory strategies are ineffective not because philosophers have proclaimed the vanity of foundations, but because emancipatory drives have been effectively privatized so that further emancipatory moves are increasingly resistant to collectivization.

The issue of the possibility of critique is ultimately resolved not in philosophical disputes, but in the social figuration which determines the shape of the life-tasks and the range of strategies these tasks demand or allow. The likelihood of critique is but loosely, if at all, related to the philosophical elegance of the proof of its legitimacy. It is, on the other hand, intimately linked to the degree to which the figuration prompts, or preempts, questioning of the rules which guide and assure its reproduction. Sociologists may therefore take little notice of philosophical blackmail; the philosophers' bid for the double status of legislators and judges was itself a product of the selfsame figuration that has been decomposed with the advent of postmodernity; it was well geared to the powers bent on global projects and global redemption, now conspicuous by their absence. Postmodernity has put the question of the feasibility of emancipatory critique firmly and squarely in the sociology court-yard.

It is in this context that one should assess the significance and practical value of Baudrillard's analyses. Sociological diagnosis of the current figuration may not by itelf guarantee reform, but without it prospects of critique would look gloomier still. It is important to know that decomposition and dissipation have taken the place of the globally managed projects, and simulacra replaced commodity fetishism in its role of the veil hiding the link between individual fate and social figuration. It is important to know that with the amazing absorptive capacity of that figuration's self-perpetuating mechanism, a change-bearing shock may come only from outside. But what is the outside of postmodernity? One may agree with Baudrillard that *il n'y a pas dehors du jeu*. But is there no outside to the assembly of players? Is everybody a player?

Baudrillard's work may be usefully read as a travelogue of a visitor to a country not all (not many?) have had so far a chance (and not all, at any realistic stretch of time, are likely to have a chance) to explore. The problem is that those who in the land now left behind used to supply the formulae of emancipatory criticism, moved massively to that other country the others do not know, and show unmistakable symptoms of settling down in their new habitat. From their new residence, those others who did not (could not, wished not to) follow them, look baffling: frightening, like *les classes dangereux* of yore, but unlike them impotent and placid: the *masses* (as distinct from *players*), whose indifference 'is their true, their only practice' (Baudrillard in Kellner 1989: 85). Of the morphology of that mysterious leftover Baudrillard has little to say – and so he flatly denies that there is a morphology to speak of. One wonders.

NOTE

1 This is what, in the end, Christopher Norris must have had in mind when he stated that 'Baudrillard is in no position to adopt such a critical stance, having argued repeatedly against the idea – the deluded "Enlightenment" idea – that we could ever think beyond this realm of false appearance to that which it supposedly dissimulates or masks' (Norris 1990: 134). Although Norris repeatedly insists that his objection to Baudrillard does not stem from sheer pragmatic concern with the guarantees of political effectivity, he, much in the spirit of the lost/ missed premise, dedicates his search to 'grounding' the *legitimacy* (rather than the *possibiliy*) of critique extraneously. Contrary to his own declared intentions, Norris reverts, however, time and again to the ground-seeker's super-charge as the clinching argument that this search is not a waste of time: Baudrillard's vision 'should bring comfort to government advisers, PR experts, campaign managers . . . and others with an interest in maintaining this state of affairs'.

REFERENCES

Baudrillard, J. (1988a) *Selected Writings*, ed. Mark Poster, Cambridge, Polity Press.
—— (1988b) *America*, trans. Chris Turner, London, Verso.

────── (1990a) *Le Transparence du mal, essai sur les phénomènes extrêmes*, Paris, Galilée.

────── (1990b) *Seduction*, trans. Brian Singer, London, Macmillan.

────── (1990c) *Cool Memories*, London, Verso.

Corbin, A. (1982) *Le Miasme et la jonquille*, Paris, Aubier.

Debord, G. (1990) *Comments on the Society of the Spectacle*, trans. Malcolm Imrie, London, Verso.

Kellner, D. (1989) *Jean Baudrillard. From Marxism to Postmodernism and Beyond*, Cambridge, Polity Press.

Lyotard, J.-F. (1991) *Le Postmoderne expliqué aux enfants*, Paris, Galilée.

Maffesoli, M. (1985) *L'Ombre de Dionysos: contribution à une sociologie de l'orgie*, Paris, Méridiens.

Norris, C. (1990) 'Lost in the funhouse: Baudrillard and the politics of postmodernism', in Roy Boyne and Ali Rattansi (eds) *Postmodernism and Society*, London, Macmillan.

Chapter 3

Europe/America
Baudrillard's fatal comparison

Barry Smart

During the course of the twentieth century 'the age of Europe' gave way to the 'heyday of American world hegemony' (West 1989: 87). Subsequently there have been changes in both the shape and the relationship between a number of geopolitical and cultural unities, changes which continue to provoke controversy and debate. It has been suggested that we are now living through 'the crisis of the Pax Americana' (Eco 1987: 76), that 'the rise of postmodern culture seems to coincide with the eclipse of America' (Wark 1990: 20), and that 'America no longer has the same hegemony, no longer enjoys the same monopoly' (Baudrillard 1988a: 116). Simultaneously there has been talk of the constitution of a 'new' Europe, a United States of Europe (Tatchell 1989), an extended Europe which would encompass the post-cold war states of both east and western regions of the 'continent' (Voigt 1989). Also on the agenda for discussion is the growing significance of a resurgent 'orient', in particular a wealthy and increasingly influential Japan, a sign perhaps of an emerging new non-territorial empire, a simulation of empire, or should it be an empire of simulations? To this by no means exhaustive list it is necessary to add the continuing movements, struggles, and conflicts besetting the Middle East, the reemergence of Arab nationalism, and the regeneration of an Islamic fundamentalism articulating criticisms of both the West and proliferating social, cultural, and political manifestations of western modernity (Watt 1988; Zubaida 1989).

The cultural and geopolitical unities referred to above are well known, but their referents are far from fixed, indeed it may be argued that they have no definitive referents, no reality beyond the discourses within which they are constituted. This does not mean that they have no existence, or that they only exist linguistically, but that there is no 'extradiscursive reality that discourse might simply reflect' (Laclau 1988: 79). A cautionary note. There is no sense here in which reality is simply being equated with language; rather my argument is that what we know as 'Europe' and 'America' is constituted through discursive relations within which linguistic and extra- and non-linguistic elements are articulated. In consequence the 'unities' Europe and America are relatively open-ended, subject to interpretation, and as a corollary, a range of meanings. They are changing unities, unities with histories, contestable unities.

The aim of my essay is to explore key features of Baudrillard's work, in particular his notion of 'theory' and its relation to the 'real', as well as his ideas on modernity and postmodernity, through an analysis of his travelogue on America. Consideration is given not only to the immediate focus of Baudrillard's narrative, namely the *novus mundus* of America, but also to the less prominent construct of 'Europe' which informs the discussion.

EUROPE/AMERICA: IMAGINARY WORLDS

When reference is made to Europe of what do we think? How are we to interpret Europe? Is it the European Economic Community, the 'Common Market', that comes to mind, that economic and political formation that has grown since 1958 to a membership of twelve states? Perhaps we envisage Gorbachev's post-cold war conception of a Europe extending from the Atlantic seaboard to the Urals, a 'common home' for the peoples of East and West. An alternative response would be to question the assumption and possibility of a unity, to reflect upon the existence of several different Europes, those (comm)unities imagined in the 'core' countries of Britain, France and Germany, as well as others constituted in smaller, in some respects more marginal countries such as Sweden, Spain, Portugal and Hungary (Enzensberger 1989).

The origin of the term Europe is open to speculation. More certain is its presence in the discourse of classical antiquity. The term Europe appears to have been initially employed in a geographical sense, to designate a 'continent' adjacent to 'Asia'. The geographical basis for partitioning an 'indivisible Eurasia' was from the beginning contentious, the subsequent fifth-century adoption of the terms 'Europe' and 'Asia' by Herodotus to describe a feud between political and cultural unities signifying an unwarranted extension of their meaning. In short there was no justification for transferring the geographical terms Europe and Asia from the 'mariner's chart to the publicist's political map and to the sociologist's diagram of the habitats of cultures' (Toynbee 1954: 710). The accumulation of anomalies and problems concerning the relevance of a categorical distinction between Europe and Asia for understanding geographic, linguistic, ecclesiastical, cultural and political differences meant that the distinction could not be sustained, and in the post-Alexandrine Age of Hellenic history it ceased to be used. The distinction between Europe and Asia was revived in the fifteenth century, in the context of the modern western Renaissance and the 'opening up [of] new worlds across the Ocean' (Toynbee 1954: 115 n. 4). When Columbus reached land in 1492 after voyaging across the Atlantic the accepted map of the world indicated that another sea route to the Orient had been discovered. The identification of a new continent, a *novus mundus*, had to await Amerigo Vespucci's intervention at the turn of the century, a contribution which received cartographic recognition in 1507 with the publication of a new world map showing a new continent *America terra* (Mason 1990: 18–19).

At the end of the seventeenth century the nautical term 'Europe' was again employed to constitute a cultural unity. However, the deployment of Europe as an alternative to 'Western Christendom' continued to be problematic.[1] The term remained a 'geographical misfit', for the western geopolitical formation which constituted itself as Europe did not correspond to the territory designated by the original Hellenic concept. In relation to the parameters of western civilization Europe was both too narrow and too broad. Too narrow adequately to cover the rapidly growing non-European cultural empire, and too broad to take account of the existence of significant cultural differences between different regions of 'the European Continent'. Europe as a synonym for the West made 'intellectual nonsense of the cultural situation in that culturally non-Western quarter of a "continent" that had no unity' (Toynbee 1954: 722). It led to the view that the cultural diversity and relative 'backwardness' of south-eastern Europe constituted a legitimate focus for the exercise of modern western power. Such an assumption has undoubtedly contributed to the 'mutual misunderstanding and ill-feeling' between the modern West and 'the contemporary Islamic and Orthodox Christian worlds' (Toynbee 1954: 722). Misunderstanding and ill-feeling which shows no sign of diminishing at present. The conclusion to which Toynbee is drawn is that by 'adopting the name "Europe" as a substitute for Western Christendom, the Modern Western World had replaced a misnomer that was merely an anachronism by a misnomer that was seriously misleading' (1954: 729). Whether as a geopolitical, economic, or cultural formation, the meaning of Europe has remained in question.

In a series of comments which parallel Toynbee's reflections on the close of the modern age of western history, Feher argues that in the post-second world war period European culture survives, but only as an exhibit:

> 'Europe' could cope neither politically nor culturally with the new forms of modernity, arising from its womb, from its own culture, each of them denying with its existence the very message in whose name the so-called 'European idea', in short, the message of the Enlightenment, had been conceived. 'Europe' had lost . . . the unassailable self-confidence which filled European hearts both on the left and the right throughout the nineteenth century. It has lost the conviction that one day, the whole of the world will be 'European' in a cultural sense.
>
> (1988: 89)

A view endorsed by Baudrillard (1988a), who argues that if Europe once seemed to constitute the cultural nucleus of modernity, it no longer retains that position. No longer as active, no longer the driving force, Europe, once considered the source and model for progress, is depicted as encumbered by tradition, by the past, lacking the modern spirit, and in consequence incapacitated in the pursuit of modernity. In contrast America is described as 'the absolute model for everyone' (p. 77), for it is 'in America and nowhere else that modernity is original' (p. 81).

It should be evident from the above that I take the view that there is 'no concrete referent to which the sign "America" should be supposed to refer. Like other proper names it is an "effect of the real", a (re)presentation' (Mason 1990: 34). From the moment at which the process of reinscription of European names on the New World occluded or eroded the traces of earlier Indian discoverers, America presented problems of description and representation. It seemed simultaneously to be 'the same and not the same' and in consequence constituted a problem for the sixteenth-century Renaissance *episteme* structured in terms of relations of resemblance and identity (Foucault 1973: 68). As Mason notes,

The way in which observers of America resorted to the world that was familiar to them is a timeless response by self when faced with the challenge of the other. In using the elements familiar to them, they were in fact engaged in a double process of reduction and construction. In *constructing* the New World, resemblance was linked with imagination to avoid the endless monotony of the same. The result is a continuing process of construction and reconstruction of a world, which we may therefore call an imaginary world. The frame of reference remains the Old World.

(Mason 1990: 25)

And the context pre-Enlightenment colonial discourse.

In a post-Enlightenment, post-colonial context observers still resort to the familiar. But now it is necessary to recognize that if America is Europe's other, Europe in its turn constitutes America's other. Furthermore, just as there is no 'essential' Europe, its reality being discursive, so 'the discourses on America, as presented in texts and images, *are* America . . . [W]e have no means at our disposal for severing the thread linking discourse to representation, no way of approaching America "as it really is", because such a notion is devoid of significance' (Mason 1990: 174).

As will become clear below, Baudrillard portrays Europe as forever chasing the shadow of America's radical otherness, but stops short of presenting the two 'unities' as wholly incommensurable. Indeed for comparisons between Europe and America to be possible at all there needs must be a degree of commensurability, the possibility of constituting at least some common reference points. However, before joining Baudrillard in America it is necessary to consider some of the idiosyncratic features of his approach to social theory and analysis.

THEORY AS CHALLENGE

Baudrillard has been described as the first to 'organise . . . a postmodern social theory' (Kellner 1988: 242). But it is arguable whether a postmodern *social* theory is present in the work, or for that matter whether such a theory can be generated from within the analytic vortex Baudrillard fabricates. Indeed given some of Baudrillard's more extravagant comments on the fate of the social it might be more appropriate to classify his œuvre as anti-social theory. Moreover, whilst it is indisputable that Baudrillard's analysis sits uneasily with the project of modernity, and further that there are a number of explicit references to postmodernity in his work, he is far from consistent in his observations on present conditions, and in the commentary on Europe and America references are almost entirely confined to the modern and modernity, about which more later.

There is no objectivity to the world that theory can promise or pretend to capture or represent in Baudrillard's view. Theory is described as having 'no status other than that of challenging the real' (Baudrillard 1987: 125). This follows from the effacement of the relationship between the real and the imaginary in and through the constitution of the 'hyperreal'. As Baudrillard argues, 'the real becomes . . . *that of which it is possible to give an equivalent reproduction* . . . . the real is not only what can be reproduced, but *that which is always already reproduced*. The hyperreal' (1983: 146). And on the question of the relationship of theory to 'the real' Baudrillard is no less enigmatic. Theory's end is no longer that accepted since the Enlightenment, namely, to represent or reflect the real, or to critically engage with the real. Such a conception of theory can no longer be sustained, for there is 'no "reality" with respect to which theory could become dissident or heretical, pursuing its fate other than in the objectivity of things. Rather, it's the objectivity of things we must question' (Baudrillard 1987: 125).

Forms of theorizing which lay claim to a privileged access to the real are no longer appropriate, no longer adequate given the prevalence of an order of simulation. The precession of simulacra means appeal cannot be made to external referents or to an objective real. Representations can no longer be compared, contrasted, and evaluated in terms of an independent real. Operational simulation dissolves 'the difference between "true" and "false", between "real" and "imaginary"' (Baudrillard 1983: 5). Nevertheless, despite repeated reformulations of such propositions – 'nothing happens in the real' (1987: 126); 'truth, reference and objective causes have ceased to exist' (1983: 6); 'reality itself today . . . is hyperrealist' (1983: 147); the 'principle of simulation wins out over the reality principle' (1983: 152) – Baudrillard's work seems to be perpetually preoccupied with the prevailing order of things, with telling it like it is, with the presentation of a discourse that corresponds somehow to the way in which the world has changed. As Morris has suggested, Baudrillard's work seductively invites the reader to respond yes, that is 'the way things *really are*' (1988b: 191). This is particularly evident in Baudrillard's observations on Europe and America.

Conventional forms of analysis assume, or claim, a possible relationship of correspondence, critique or even transformation between theory and reality. Baudrillard comments that this has never been his position, theory cannot be reconciled with the real either in a relationship of 'truthful' affirmation or 'negational' critique. Theory we are told 'becomes an event in and of itself' (1987: 127), its status that of a 'challenge to the real' (1988b: 98). A challenge that seems to be bound up with a notion of 'fatality', with a strategy that involves siding with the object, recognizing 'that there is a fatal and enigmatic bias in the order of things' (1990a: 191). Because objects and their effects consistently overflow our conceptions, explanations, expectations and anticipations, there is a need for a theoretical strategy which forces things 'into an over-existence which is incompatible with that of the real' (1988b: 98). Theory following a fatal strategy has to force things to their extremity, and beyond, literally it has 'to defy the world to be more' (1988b: 100). And 'more' as Eco (1987: 8) reminds us is an intrinsic feature of American hyperreality.

EUROPE'S OTHER: TRAVELLERS' TALES

Baudrillard is not the only contemporary European intellectual who has sought to reflect upon the hyperreality of America. Umberto Eco has also sought to explore the 'furious hyperreality' of America, to describe American taste and mentality, and to offer brief observations on America's 'other', Europe. America is said to be obsessed with realism, with the construction of perfect replicas, 'real' copies, or 'authentic' representations. Eco argues that the production of full-scale copies 'dominates the relation with the self, with the past, not infrequently with the present, always with History and, even, with the European tradition' (1987: 6). Preoccupied with 'the real thing', the American imagination increasingly resorts to simulations which dissolve the boundaries between 'true' and 'false', 'reality' and 'reproduction'. Reconstructions and fusions of 'copy and original' abound, creating a spatio-temporal haze where virtually everything appears present.

The American preoccupation with a 'ravenous consumption of the present and constant "past-ising" process' (Eco 1987: 9),

museumification, and simulation of an 'authentic' real is evident in
the pervasiveness of reproductions of the past, collections of
antiques, and other forms of historical reconstruction garbed in a
fake authenticity. It is worth adding that the philosophy of hyperrealism also effectively dissolves conventional distinctions between
'real' and 'possible' worlds, between realities and fantasies. The
presence of 'fakes' alongside 'authentic' artefacts in museums and
galleries, and in turn the 'authenticity' ascribed to historical fakes
leads Eco to ruminate on the way in which mementoes and antiques
'plundered from half of Europe' might be viewed by future
observers 'ignorant of a Europe long since vanished'. The articulation of fake and authentic artefacts is held by Eco to bring us 'to
the theme of the Last Beach, the apocalyptic philosophy that more
or less explicitly rules these reconstructions: Europe is declining
into barbarism and something has to be saved' (1987: 36). An
ironic observation, for if the 'Old World' of Europe has indeed
been in relative decline since the end of the second world war it has
until relatively recently been a result of economic and cultural
colonization by the 'New World' of America (1987: 39). Furthermore, if the survival of European civilization, however that might
be conceived, has been in question, it has been for the most part
because of the perpetuation of a climate of 'cold war' and an
associated process of escalating 'defence' expenditure and military
rearmament, for which successive American administrations must
carry a major share of responsibility. It is hardly surprising that
Europe's artefacts and treasures have been identified as in need of
collection and preservation given that, before the era of *glasnost*
and *perestroika* and the associated revolutions of 1989 in Eastern
Europe, American foreign policy and military strategy were predicated on simulations which assumed the expendability of a central
European 'theatre', if not of Europe itself.

If Eco's journey through the hyperreality of America ultimately
reveals the outline of a critical understanding of key features of the
times in which we live, specifically that we are witnessing an
erosion, if not a collapse of American hegemony, Baudrillard's
narrative, in contrast, for the most part reads like a homage to
America, one which oscillates between a celebratory phenomenological excursion through the (hyper)reality of the 'New World',
and an intermittent and dislocated comparative analysis of European and American *modernity*. But the America Baudrillard
presents is one seen (scene) through (on) the screen of his car

(cinema). One journey, one route, one form of travel, and one vision. There are other possibilities, possibilities which would have allowed Baudrillard to experience different Americas:

> He could easily have taken a slow train south from Minneapolis and followed the Mississippi river to New Orleans. Another version of the country would have revealed itself: the erotic rhythm of the rails, faded Amtrak coaches filled with boozy blacks, microwave dinners, Japanese tourists with Walkmans, conductors calling out Memphis in the early morning and pointing to Graceland, urban and rural landscapes painted in Edward Hopper colours, all-night diners, country-western music, New Orleans jazz, the bayou country with the cajuns, bridges which extend forever over waterways that run to the Gulf of Mexico . . . But American trains aren't for European travellers and Baudrillard wasn't in search of this version of America.
>
> (Denzin 1991: 125)

Baudrillard arrived already in possession of his America, possessed by it, a colonized subject of its empire of cinematic signs.

Baudrillard's America is the desert. As he confesses, '[my] hunting grounds are the deserts, the mountains, Los Angeles, the freeways, the Safeways, the ghost towns, or the downtowns, not lectures at the university' (1988a: 63). It is more than a little ironic that the central metaphor running through Baudrillard's travelogue on America should be that of the desert. For in the wake of the Gulf war the articulation of America and the desert has a new resonance. Moreover, contrary to Baudrillard's controversial comments on the 'corpse of war' and the associated prediction that 'the Gulf war will not happen' (1991: 25), America became deeply involved in a desert conflict, locked into what appeared, in some respects at least, to be a high technology secular equivalent to the military crusades conducted in the eleventh, twelfth, and thirteenth centuries (Watt 1988: 17). Where the crusaders sought to bring the holy places of Christianity under Christian order and control, the United Nations American-led campaign had as its proclaimed primary objective restoration of the sovereign order of a western-designated modern nation state. The claim has been made that the complex events associated with the ending of the occupation of Kuwait by Iraq also confirm the beginning of a 'new world order', one guaranteed by the military prowess of the sole remaining 'superpower'. If in the immediate afterglow of operation 'Desert

Storm' the possibility of an American-led 'new world order' appeared to be confirmed, subsequent events that 'a large measure of disorder, loose ends, [and] untidy arrangements' (Sommer 1991) will remain a corollary. In other words, if a new order is emerging it is articulated with both persisting and newly emerging forms of disorder. Moreover, the kinds of 'America' that might materialize from the complex articulation of continuing transformations in culture, politics, and social and economic life in a post-cold war context, and the place and role that America might assume in any new emerging global order or configuration are far from predetermined or guaranteed.

The identification of America with the desert occurs in several different contexts in Baudrillard's narrative. Not surprisingly there are a number of references to the deserts of the American West, in particular to the difficulty of conceiving of the desert independently of its cinematic aspects. As Baudrillard remarks, 'those features are thoroughly superimposed upon it and will not go away. The cinema has absorbed everything – Indians, *mesas*, canyons, skies' (1988a: 69). But there are other deserts in Baudrillard's text, the desert as 'indifferent', 'emptiness', 'space', 'silence', and 'ecstatic critique of culture' (p. 5). Indeed deserts seem, at times, to be virtually everywhere. As Baudrillard declares,

> I know the deserts, their deserts, better than they do . . . I get to know more about the concrete social life of America from the desert than I ever would from official or intellectual gatherings.
>
> American culture is heir to the deserts, but the deserts here are not part of a Nature defined by contrast with the town. Rather they denote the emptiness, the radical nudity that is the background to every human institution. At the same time, they designate human institutions as a metaphor of that emptiness and the work of man as the continuity of the desert, culture as a mirage and as the perpetuity of the simulacrum.
>
> (1988a: 63)

In brief, desert as metaphysic, as 'other' to the excess of 'signification, of intention and pretention in culture'.

In contrast to the cities of Europe, American cities are described as having no monuments, no history, as being 'mobile deserts' (p. 123), indifferent and depthless. Differences which it might be argued follow from *desertum*, literally the effective severing of links between the Old and New Worlds, from the fact that whilst

European societies were embroiled in revolutionary forms of change in the course of the nineteenth century, America 'kept intact – preserved as it was by a breadth of ocean that created something akin to temporal insularity – the utopian and moral perspective of the man of the eighteenth century, or even the Puritan sects of the seventeenth, transplanted and kept alive, safely sheltered from the vicissitudes of history' (p. 90). The clear implication of which is that the physical and cultural disarticulation following emigration facilitated the realization of a radical modernity, the achievement of a way of life that now constitutes, in Baudrillard's view, the model of modernity.

NOT THE REAL THING

It has been suggested that Baudrillard went to America, 'Tocqueville in postmodern garb, to reinscribe the large mythologies, and to insist upon their essential correctness' (Buhle 1990: 166). Whatever the intention, the observations offered continually invoke European realities and in many instances draw categorical contrasts between Europe and America. Indeed Baudrillard goes so far as to assert that there is an 'unbridgeable rift' between America and Europe (1988a: 73), a comment which raises interesting questions about the possibility of realizing the kind of high level comparative exercise attempted.

America is indisputably a narrative of a European fascinated by America. Immense skies, turbulent city streets, and space on the 'grand scale' are contrasted with their diminished European equivalents. European thoughts are described, like the skies and the clouds, as 'fleecy', as 'never thoughts of wide open spaces' (1988a: 16). One possible implication of this is that geographical, architectural, and demographic features have necessary cultural and cognitive corollaries. But comments of this order are not really worthy of serious consideration. At best they serve to demonstrate the proposition that at times European thoughts may indeed be woolly! Further comparisons between Europe and America on questions of space, history, and culture lead Baudrillard to the ecologically precise observation that 'Europe has never been a continent', and to the experientially expressive comment that as soon as you land in America 'you feel the presence of an entire continent – space there is the very form of thought' (p. 16). But ultimately it is questions of modernity that are at the heart of

Baudrillard's comparison of Europe and America, and it is to these specifically that I will address my comments.

Europe is described by Baudrillard as peripheral, marginal, constantly and unavoidably trailing in the wake of America, predestined to find all-out modernity beyond its reach. Unable to realize its historical ideals Europe is portrayed as in a state of crisis, as lacking a dynamic common spirit and culture, and as facing difficulties in its attempt to construct a federal political structure. Modernity in Europe is represented as 'anachronistic', and 'lacklustre', whilst in contrast America is said to exemplify 'the absolute model for everyone' (1988a: 77), to be the very embodiment of modernity. Moreover, as hard as Europe might strive to emulate America it is asserted that there will remain a 'whole chasm of modernity' between the two, because:

> . . . you are born modern, you do not become so. *And we have never become so.* What strikes you immediately in Paris is that you are in the nineteenth century. Coming from Los Angeles, you land back in the 1800s. Every country bears a sort of historical predestination, which almost definitively determines its characteristics. For us, it is the bourgeois model of 1789 . . . that shapes our landscape. There is nothing we can do about it: everything here revolves around the nineteenth-century bourgeois dream.
>
> (p. 73)

A comment which is interesting not only for what it addresses but also for what it avoids, namely any recognition of the continuing significance within contemporary America of the events associated with the American Revolution and the Declaration of Independence, as well as the impact of the same on the cultural and political milieu of the subsequent French Revolution and its aftermath, a connection made concrete with the erection in 1885 of the gift from France of a statue personifying liberty. The 'us' is also problematic, given Baudrillard's remarks on the difficulties currently encountered in the attempt to constitute a sense of European community.

Europe is portrayed as burdened with its traditions, preoccupied with the residues and continuing resonance of 'fedualism, aristocracy, bourgeoisie, ideology and revolution' (1988a: 80). The prospects for European unity are deemed to be obstructed by historical processes of centralization which have led to the formation of distinctive national and cultural unities; these, in turn, are said to make 'both downward diversification and upward federation equally impossible' (p. 83). In contrast a decentralized and pluralistic America is considered to be unified through a conviction, shared by Americans and others alike, that it has succeeded in realizing its foundational premises, 'that it is the realisation of everything . . . others have dreamt of – justice, plenty, rule of law, wealth, freedom' (p. 77). In short, whereas in Europe there is much agonizing over ideals and baulking at their realization, in America the real is built out of ideas, ideas are quite literally real-ized. To that extent America is described by Baudrillard as 'utopia achieved', but it is an increasingly troubled utopia, one uncertain of its duration and permanence, a complex and potentially fragile unity composed of a multiplicity of cultures, nationalities, rivalries and conflicts, one that faces the prospect of its displacement from the centre of the world stage. An America disturbed by signs of another empire, signs embodied in the figure 'Japan', a 'fictive nation' (Barthes 1987; Melville 1989) which has been described as 'the last stage of a social model envisaged first by the modern West' (Miyoshi and Harootunian, 1989: xiii; Ivy 1989).

While there is a brief reference in Baudrillard's narrative to the potential of Japan to out-perform, fascinate and disturb America in the pursuit of things modern, it is America that is presented as the 'real thing' and Europe as merely 'the dubbed or subtitled version' of modernity. In Europe we are

> . . . stuck in the old rut of worshipping difference; this leaves us with a great handicap when it comes to radical modernity, which is founded on the absence of difference. Only very reluctantly do we become modern and indifferent . . . This is why our understandings lack the modern spirit. We do not even have the *evil genius* of modernity, that genius which pushes innovation to the point of extravagance and in so doing rediscovers a kind of fantastical liberty.
>
> (Baudrillard 1988a: 97)

The die is cast. The break which led to the constitution of America simultaneously provided the preconditions for the development of a radical modernity which is beyond Europe. America lives in a perpetual present, in 'perpetual simulation, in a perpetual present of signs' (p. 76). Europe, preoccupied with origins, authenticity, traditions, and founding truths, is a 'culture of intimacy which produces manners and affectations' (p. 94), a 'culture' whose values are in question, if not in crisis, a culture which will never be able to achieve 'all-out modernity'. A conclusion which follows irresistibly from Baudrillard's observation that today 'all the myths of modernity are American' (p. 81).

MODERNITY/POSTMODERNITY

> All that is solid melts into air (Marx and Engels)
> All that is solid melts into glass (Jencks)
> All that is real becomes simulation (Baudrillard)

I have suggested that Baudrillard'a *America* spirals around an unsystematic cross-cultural comparison of Europe and America on the question of modernity. Noticeably absent from the narrative is any sustained consideration of that form of life, postmodernity, generally identified with Baudrillard's work. There is, as far as I can tell, only one brief quizzical reference to the postmodern in the whole text, and that occurs in an ecstatic essay on California. Describing the Bonaventure Hotel, the revolving cocktail bar, the 'labyrinthine convolution' of the interior of the hotel, and associated illusory effects, Baudrillard asks, 'Ludic and hallucinogenic, is this postmodern architecture?' (1988a: 59). Given the 'semantic inflation' (Jencks 1990) from which our age already suffers, it is perhaps understandable that there might be doubts about whether the question warrants an answer. However, whatever the answer, it is worth bearing in mind that Baudrillard appears to have temporarily abandoned the *conceptual* distinction between a nineteenth-century revolution of 'modernity' involving 'the radical destruction of appearances . . . [and] disenchantment of the world', and a twentieth-century revolution of 'post-modernity' synonymous with a 'destruction of meaning, equal to the earlier destruction of appearances' (1984a: 38–9), for a contrast between 'modernity' and 'radical modernity'.

Another cautionary note. Contributions to the debate over the notions of modernity and postmodernity are frequently overblown. At times it seems as though contributors are more concerned to protect existing intellectual capital and 'keep the faith', than to give appropriate consideration to the range of issues and problems involved. And in view of possible misunderstandings which might arise from my comment about the absence of any sustained explicit address of the question of postmodernity in *America*, it is worth remembering that the 'postmodern', in any event, may be considered a part of the 'modern' (Lyotard 1986). Indeed, such a relationship appears to be implied in Baudrillard's relatively brief explicit comments on the subject, for example

> ... we live on like weary commentators on that frenzied period in which the whole invention of modernity . . . occurred in a language which still bore the brilliance of style . . . There is something like a general entropic movement in the century, the initial energy dissipating slowly in the sophisticated ramifications of the structural, pictural, ideological, linguistic and psychoanalytic revolutions – the final configuration, that of 'postmodernity' marking the most degraded, most factitious, and most eclectic phase.
>
> (1990b: 149–50)

And later, 'Postmodernity is the simultaneity of the destruction of earlier values and their reconstruction. It is renovation within ruination' (p. 171).

I am not convinced of the marked conceptual shift from modernity to postmodernity that some critics find in the development of Baudrillard's work. Indeed I believe that such a reading runs the risk of organizing and systematizing comments and observations that are singularly lacking in such qualities. To that extent I take a different view from Doug Kellner who suggests that Baudrillard 'interprets the rise of the system of objects and consumer society under the sign of *modernity* (whereas later he will describe the genesis and contours of what he will eventually call a "postmodern" world)' (1989: 9). In my view Baudrillard's work does not provide a clearly articulated notion of a postmodern world, or for that matter an understanding of 'what a post-modern culture would be' (1984b: 20). I am, in consequence, more inclined towards Kellner's subsequent reassessment, namely that in his 1980s texts 'Baudrillard continues to use the term "modernity" as the global framework of his analysis, and the few times that he mentions a "postmodern" phenomenon, he tends to be a bit churlish and critical, and so far has resisted spelling out a theory of postmodernity' (Kellner 1989: 121).

The continuing importance of 'modernity' as a focus for Baudrillard's deliberations is well demonstrated in the comparisons drawn between Europe and America, comparisons which signify that it is in America that simulation has achieved its most developed state and that things American constitute 'the ideal material for an anlysis of all the possible variants of the modern world' (1988a: 29).[2] Indeed if there is a consistent continuous thread running through *America*, it is that Europe and America are radically different. Cultural distinctions and qualities considered meaningful in Europe are deemed to be inappropriate, or of no relevance in America. However, as I have noted above, there is both the clear implication of a basis on which the two might be compared, and in addition an assumption that the (hyper)reality of America is understandable to a European observer, a cultural outsider. Taking Baudrillard at his word, a dangerous ploy, it would appear that 'the *truth* of America can only be seen by a European, since [s]he alone will discover here the perfect simulacrum – that of the immanence and material transcription of all values' (p. 28, emphasis added). So, while in one sense 'beyond us all', America is nevertheless portrayed as accessible to an intrepid European traveller, *un étranger* with Euro-vision. However, in view of Baudrillard's related observations on the imposing presence of significant cultural differences, the quality of both access and associated understandings is open to question.

In a series of comments which parallel some of the features intrinsic to phenomenological sociologies of everyday life, Baudrillard remarks that if you really want to know about America then you have to get in a car and drive, that way you will 'learn more about this society than all academia could ever tell you', more 'than all the institutes of sociology and political science put together' (pp. 54, 55). But the potential learning experience available to the mobile phenomenological subject is itself simultaneously problematized by the parallel identification of what are presented as significant cultural differences which derive from such 'fundamental determinants' of everyday social life in America as the experience of space and pace, mobility and flux, and the screen (TV/cinematic) and its attendant refractions (pp. 54, 55).

Cultural characteristics are articulated in a number of different ways in *America*, but virtually all of them draw on the metaphor of the desert. Consider, for example, the following – 'Culture, politics – and sexuality too – are seen exclusively in terms of the desert, which here assumes the status of a primal scene' (p. 28) and later, 'the whole of America is a desert. Culture exists there in a wild state: it sacrifices all intellect, all aesthetics in a process of literal transcription in the real' (p. 99). The contrast implied is between

'the high flown rhetoric and theatricality of our [read European]
bourgeois cultures' (p. 100) and a culture without pathos, sentiment, and heritage, a culture constituted by Baudrillard as a clear-
ing within which European aesthetic demands and cultural values
have no place. But such cultural constraints evidently do not inhibit
analysis, for Baudrillard is able to assert that,

> Banality, lack of culture, and vulgarity do not have the same
> meaning here as they have in Europe . . . The fact is that a
> certain banality, a certain vulgarity which seems unacceptable to
> us in Europe seem more than acceptable – even fascinating – to
> us here. The fact is that all our analyses in terms of alienation,
> conformism, standardisation and dehumanisation collapse of
> themselves: when we look at America it is the analyses which
> seem vulgar.

(1988a: 102)

The very possibility of such cross-cultural comparisons and the
subsequent identification of differences between Europe and
America indicate the presence of a common referent, a foundation
or ground for analysis. That common ground is clearly modernity
as a way of life, portrayed as already realized in America and
eagerly pursued in Europe. A way of life which provides the necessary preconditions for the analytic practices which Baudrillard
pushes to the limit.

The identification of radical modernity with the American way
of life and its culture of 'space, speed, cinema, technology' and the
parallel observation that international style has become American,
that American culture has become a universal model, lead Baudrillard to argue that 'Europe can no longer be understood by starting
out from Europe itself' (1988a: 98), and subsequently to conclude
that 'the key to Europe is not to be found in its past history, but in
this crazy, parodic anticipation that is the New World' (p. 104).
Given the importance Baudrillard attaches to history and tradition
in explaining the radically different dispositions towards modernity
evidenced in Europe and America, such a conclusion is, to say the
least, puzzling. So too is the total lack of any consideration of the
relationship between processes of global diffusion and economic
and cultural forms of imperialism which might account for the continuing prominence of American culture (Smith 1990), and the
neglect of the dark side of the 'American Dream', the evidence of
'long-term decline, faltering living standards, a crisis of profitability

in the nonfinancial sector [and] . . . signs of financial fragility' (Cockburn 1988: 103). Furthermore, the comments offered on European and American modernity suggest a radical shift, or at least the possibility of a serious inconsistency, in Baudrillard's conception of the relationship between 'theory' and the 'real', virtually an acceptance of a point or moment of exchange between the two that is fundamentally at odds with the notion that theory can only be a challenge to the real (1987, 1988b). Problems, absences, and inconsistencies of this order lend credence to the view that, read as a whole, *America* may be 'symptomatic of the decline of Baudrillard's theoretical powers' (Kellner 1989: 170).

However, it would be inappropriate to convey a totally negative impression, for there are many interesting, provocative and, para-doxical as it may sound, revelatory observations in Baudrillard's work (Poster 1990). One observation which has a particular signifi-cance in present circumstances is that 'Americans fight with two essential weapons: air power and information. That is, with physical bombardment of the enemy and the electronic bombard-ment of the rest of the world' (1988a: 49). Baudrillard's reference is to the Vietnam war, but the comment is equally, if not more applic-able to that war which former American President George Bush promised would not be another Vietnam, that is the Gulf war, a war of which it has been said that it was 'sometimes hard to tell the real thing from an arcade simulation' (Greenfield 1991). Baudril-lard's (1983) challenging comments on the 'hyperrealism of simula-tion' clearly have something to say to us in a context where 'George Bush and Saddam Hussein are actors on video and the weaponry is fired via satellite' (Sampson 1990: 24). But pursuing a fatal strategy, pushing ideas to their limit, to their extremity, led Baudrillard, once more, to over-reach and to chance the prediction that 'US might and . . . western power in general . . . has . . . been cowed and paralysed by its own strength. It is incapable of using its position within the balance of power. That is why the Gulf War will not happen' (1991: 25). Siding with the object is always risky, as Baudrillard acknowledges, but in this instance, unfortunately, it was not only the 'fatal strategy' that proved to be truly fatal.

In Baudrillard's view theory 'does not derive its legitimacy from established facts, but from future events. Its value is not in the past events it can illuminate, but in the shockwave of the events it pre-figures' (1990b: 215). That is why theory is considered to constitute a challenge to the real. But in so far as events remain 'indifferent' to our prefiguring it is evident that the real constitutes a challenge to theory (Baudrillard 1988b). Our fate is to be abroad in a universe that refuses to submit to our designs, a universe that continues to be an enigma. Our theories do not lay bare the objective order of things, but rather contribute in direct and indirect ways to ongoing complex processes of transformation and, to that extent, challenge the real, 'defy the world to be more' (1988b: 100). In turn the impact of unintended consequences and the reflexivity of social knowledge contribute to what is experienced as the 'erratic character of modernity' (Giddens 1990: 152), the real that constitutes a challenge to modern theory.

CONCLUDING REMARKS – WHY AMERICA? WHY NOT JAPAN?

Pursuing the enigma of modernity, that form of life represented as destined to remain forever 'lacklustre' in Europe, led Baudrillard to go west, to America, the home of 'radical modernity', the source of all the myths of modernity. Baudrillard, like Kristeva, Sollers and Marcellin (Moi 1987) before him, finds the key to Europe in the United States. But does the key still fit? In a context where it has been suggested that we are living through 'the twilight of American hegemony' (Wark 1990), that America is in 'crisis' (Eco 1987), we might wonder why Baudrillard did not follow Barthes (1987) and head east, to the empire of simulations, to the place described as 'already a satellite of the planet Earth' (Baudrillard 1988a: 76), that is to Japan.

The 'American Century' is drawing to a close and not only in a chronological sense. The shift away from Fordist organized, industrial capitalist forms of production and towards neo-Fordist, or 'Sonyist', post-industrial capitalist, more flexible forms of accumulation (Harvey 1989) is articulated with an erosion of American economic might and the emergence of new centres of influence. Is it a coincidence that the growth of postmodern culture appears to be articulated with the decline of America? (Wark 1990). Not if we are persuaded that the cultural contradictions besetting contemporary American capitalism have been aggravated by the development of postmodern forms (Bell 1976). And not if we suspect that 'Japan' might be the invigorating source of a developing postmodern capitalism, and/or accept that we are, to an extent, living through the 'Japanization' of the West anticipated by Kojève (1969: 159–62). Given the notion of postmodernism with which Baudrillard sometimes chooses to play fits 'Japanese conditions remarkably well, as if the term were coined specifically for Japanese society' (Miyoshi 1989: 148), the absence of any sustained consideration of Japan in his work is intriguing. Is it perhaps because the theorist pursuing a fatal strategy can only 'side with the object' (Baudrillard 1990a: 190) that is already known or familiar?

European experiences, understandings and identities have been substantially influenced by American social, economic, and cultural forms and practices. Baudrillard's *America* is a testimony to the complex legacy of American cultural and economic imperialism and in so far as it presents Europe as chasing the shadow of America's modernity it illustrates the continuing seductiveness of the American way. But the idea that America is the cultural, economic, and political centre of modernity is increasingly in question. Other 'diverging varients of modernity' (Arnason 1987: 8) are now recognized. In particular America's other 'other', Japan, is considered to be radically different, to exemplify 'a constellation of economic, political and cultural structures that can legitimately be described as a distinctive pattern of modernity' (Arnason 1987/1988: 56); to be 'one of a kind', a civilization which 'undertook ways diametrically opposed to the "American way"' (Kojève 1969: 161); and to have successfully avoided western techno-cultural colonization by colonizing 'technology from the fictive position of its own culture, the world's first "post"-culture' (Callas 1991: 21). Baudrillard's vision of modernity appears indifferent to such differences; indifferent to the possibility that America may no longer be the model for business, performance and international style, no longer the 'uncontested and uncontestable' model of modernity.

Moreover, it is not only America's status as the model of modernity that is now in dispute, but the very idea itself of a model of modernity. Baudrillard avoids the challenge implied here to western modernity. Focusing on America and Europe Baudrillard neglects the question of Japan and fails thereby to respond to the 'postmodern' challenge presented by the global articulation of locally inflected forms of modernity.

NOTES

1 See also Mann's (1988) contribution to a conference held on 'The European Miracle'. Mann, echoing Toynbee, asks 'Why is "Europe" to be regarded as a continent in the first place? This is not an ecological but a social fact . . . Its continental identity was primarily Christian, for its name was Christendom more often than it was Europe' (p. 10).

2 Further confirmation is provided by Baudrillard's comment that,

> For us moderns and ultramoderns, as for Baudelaire, who knew that the secret of true modernity was to be found in artifice, the only natural spectacle that is really gripping is the one which offers both the most moving profundity *and at the same time the total simulacrum of that profundity*.
>
> (1988a: 70)

REFERENCES

Arnason, J. P. (1987) 'The modern constellation and the Japanese enigma – Part I', *Thesis Eleven* 17.

—— (1987/88) 'The modern constellation and the Japanese enigma – Part II', *Thesis Eleven* 18/19.

Barthes, R. (1987) *Empire of Signs*, New York, Hill and Wang.

Baudrillard, J. (1983) *Simulations*, New York, Semiotext(e).

—— (1984a) 'On nihilism', *On the Beach* 6, Spring.

—— (1984b) 'Game with vestiges', *On the Beach* 5, Winter.

—— (1987) *Forget Foucault and Forget Baudrillard*, New York, Semiotext(e).

—— (1988a) *America*, London, Verso.

—— (1988b) *The Ecstasy of Communication*, New York, Semiotext(e).

—— (1990a) *Fatal Strategies*, New York, Semiotext(e)/Pluto.

—— (1990b) *Cool Memories*, London, Verso.

—— (1991) 'The Reality Gulf' *Guardian*, January 11.

Bell, D. (1976) *The Cultural Contradictions of Capitalism*, New York, Basic Books.

Buhle, P. (1990) 'America: post-modernity?', *New Left Review* 180, March/April.

Callas, P. (1991) 'Japan: post-department store . . . post-culture', *Tension* 25, March/April.

Cockburn, A. (1988) *Corruptions of Empire: Life Studies and the Reagan Era*, London, Verso.

Denzin, N. K. (1991) '*Paris, Texas* and Baudrillard on America', *Theory, Culture and Society* 8(2).

Eco, U. (1987) *Travels in Hyperreality*, London, Picador.

Enzensberger, H. (1989) *Europe, Europe*, London, Radius.

Feher, F. (1988) 'The Pyrrhic victory of art in its war of liberation: remarks on the postmodernist intermezzo', in A. Milner *et al.* (eds) *Postmodern Conditions*, Centre for General and Comparative Literature Publications, Monash University.

Foucault, M. (1973) *The Order of Things: An Archaeology of the Human Sciences*, New York, Vintage Books.

Giddens, A. (1990) *The Consequences of Modernity*, Cambridge, Polity Press.

Greenfield, J. (1991) *ABC Television News*, January 23, New York.

Harvey, D. (1989) *The Condition of Postmodernity*, Oxford, Blackwell.

Ivy, M. (1989) 'Critical texts, mass artifacts: the consumption of knowledge in postmodern Japan', in M. Myoshi and H. D. Harootunian (eds) *Postmodernism and Japan*, London, Duke University Press.

Jencks, C. (1990) *The New Moderns: From Late to Neo-Modernism*, London, Academy Editions.

Kellner, D. (1988) 'Postmodernism as social theory: some challenges and problems', *Theory, Culture and Society* 5(2–3).

——— (1989) *Jean Baudrillard: From Marxism to Postmodernism and Beyond*, Cambridge, Polity Press.

Kojève, A. (1969) *Introduction to the Reading of Hegel*, ed. A. Bloom, London, Basic Books.

Laclau, E. (1988) 'Politics and the limits of modernity', in A. Ross (ed.) *Universal Abandon? The Politics of Postmodernism*, Minneapolis, University of Minnesota Press.

Lyotard, J. F. (1986) *The Postmodern Condition: A Report on the Condition of Knowledge*, Manchester, Manchester University Press.

Mann, M. (1988) 'European development: approaching a historical explanation', in J. Baechler *et al.* (eds) *Europe and the Rise of Capitalism*, Oxford, Blackwell.

Mason, P. (1990) *Deconstructing America: Representations of the Other*, London, Routledge.

Melville, S. (1989) 'Picturing Japan: reflections on the workshop', in M. Miyoshi and H. D. Harootunian (eds) *Postmodernism and Japan*, London, Duke University Press.

Miyoshi, M. (1989) 'Against the native grain: the Japanese novel and the "postmodern" West', in M. Myoshi and H. D. Harootunian (eds) *Postmodernism and Japan*, London, Duke University Press.

Miyoshi, M. and Harootunian, H. D. (eds) (1989) *Postmodernism and Japan*, London, Duke University Press.

Moi, T. (ed.) (1987) *The Kristeva Reader*, Oxford, Blackwell.

Morris, M. (1988) *The Pirate's Fiancée: Feminism, Reading, Postmodernism*, London, Verso.

Poster, M. (1990) *The Mode of Information: Poststructuralism and Social Context*, Cambridge, Polity Press.

Sampson, J. (1990) 'The world's a stooge', *Tension* 23, October–November.

Smith, A. D. (1990) 'Towards a global culture?', *Theory, Culture and Society* 7(2–3).

Sommer, T. (1991) 'A world beyond order and control', *The Guardian Weekly* 44(17).

Tatchell, P. (1989) 'United States of Europe', *New Socialist* 59.

Toynbee, A. (1954) *A Study of History*, vol. VIII, London, Oxford University Press.

Voigt, K. (1989) 'New thinking, fresh hope', *New Socialist* 59.

Wark, M. (1990) 'America is dead: the tyranny of difference', *Tension* 23, October/November.

Watt, W. M. (1988) *Islamic Fundamentalism and Modernity*, London, Routledge.

West, C. (1989) 'Black culture and postmodernism', in B. Kruger and P. Mariani (eds) *Remaking History*, Seattle, Dia Art Foundation, Bay Press.

Zubaida, S. (1989) *Islam, the People and the State*, London, Routledge.

Chapter 4

Baudrillard for sociologists

Bryan S. Turner

INTRODUCTION

If the object of study of sociology is, in a rather general and loose fashion, 'the social', then the recent prophetic announcements of the death of the social necessarily involve the end of sociology. It is perhaps for this reason that professional sociologists have begun to take some notice of the work of Jean Baudrillard. With his characteristically terse, epigrammatic style, Baudrillard has pronounced that

> Sociology can only depict the expansion of the social and its vicissitudes. It survives only on the positive and definitive hypothesis of the social. The reabsorption the implosion of the social escapes it. The hypothesis of the death of the social is also that of its own death.

(1983: 4)

Within this framework of the history of the sociological discipline, 'the social' as a separately constituted terrain first emerged in the 1890s at precisely that point in western history when the academic discipline of sociology was articulated by Emile Durkheim, Max Weber and Georg Simmel. For Durkheim, the science of sociology was a separate discipline which was precisely formulated to grasp social facts, which were seen to be objective, independent and causally significant. More exactly, sociology was a science of moral facts, which would replace the individualistic doctrine of ethical life which was the legacy of Kant (Durkheim 1992). For writers like Baudrillard, in so far as the mass, in a society of global and extended consumption, has replaced 'the social', then sociology becomes a museum-piece of the academic field, at best an archaeology of the bones of the modern social fabric. There is obviously an important parallel here between Neitzsche's impact on nineteenth-century moral philosophy and theology in the apocalyptic declaration that 'God is dead', and the late twentieth-century view that 'the social is dead' (Stauth and Turner 1988: 226).

Of course, it is not just Baudrillard who has been prominent in announcing the death of traditional sociology as a science of the social. The idea of sociology as an empirical science of the social world whose aim is to produce law-like statements about social regularities has been challenged by social theorists who, inspired by the deconstructive techniques of Jacques Derrida, argue that sociology must become a deconstructive reading of the social as a collection of texts. In this case, the imperialistic claims of sociology to have a privileged access to the social are displaced by a new interdisciplinarity in which sociological readings are placed alongside literary and cultural readings of the Social Text. This deconstructive sociology involves an 'undoing of the social' (Game 1991).

This questioning of the traditional claims of sociology to be a science of the social cannot be divorced from the more general impact of postmodern theory on the social sciences and in particular on sociology in the 1980s. Although the idea about postmodernism in architecture was established, according to Charles Jencks (1977), by the death of architectural modernism in 1972, the implications of postmodernism for social theory were not fully realized until the English translation of Jean-François Lyotard's *The Postmodern Condition* (1984) and the publication of Frederic Jameson's seminal essay on 'Postmodernism, or the cultural logic of late capitalism' (1984). By the late 1980s, there was a tidal flood of expository works on postmodernism. The publishing boom of postmodernism has shown no abatement in the 1990s (Bauman 1992; Lash 1990; Smart 1992; Turner 1990).

The problematic relationship between sociology and postmodernism will be partly explored in this chapter, but we can for introductory purposes summarize the issue quite succinctly. If sociology was pre-eminently the study of modern society (that is, the study of western industrial society after the transition of European societies from agrarian feudalism to urban, industrial capitalism) as originally formulated in the sociological ideas of Karl Marx, Auguste Comte, Claude St. Simon and Herbert Spencer, then the claim that we are living in a postmodern epoch suggests, at the very least, that sociology is hopelessly ill-equipped to comprehend this transition. The galaxy of sociological concepts which was forged to understand the social realities of industrial society – social class, social differentiation, anomie, ideology, status, alienation and so forth – has to be consigned to the dustbin of the history of ideas. A new vocabulary – society as spectacle, simulacra, fatal strategies, the hyperreal, emotive tribes, impolsion, the imaginary and so forth – offers an alternative discourse by which the complexities of the new realm of postmodernity might be approached. Although as we will see, it is probably inaccurate to suggest that Baudrillard is a postmodern thinker (Gane 1991a: 48), his name has become inextricably tied up with postmodernism with the result that many commentators have come to assume that Baudrillard's critique of sociology as a science of the social is in fact *the* postmodern attack.

The response to both Baudrillard and postmodernism in mainstream sociology has so far been less than adequate. For many the response has been one of frustration, anger and disappointment (Callinicos 1989; Kellner 1989a and 1989b; Vidich 1991). Perhaps the only systematic and sympathetic guide has been produced by Mike Gane (1991a and 1991b). However, the complex task of sorting out the problems of a postmodern sociology versus a sociology of postmodernism has hardly begun (Featherstone 1991). In this chapter, I am concerned to try to formulate the epistemological and theoretical challenge of postmodernism to conventional understandings of the tasks of sociology, on the one hand, and a sympathetic commentary on Baudrillard with special reference to the debate about America (Baudrillard 1989), on the other.

Some preliminary ground-clearing comments in order to sharpen the discussion are in order. Firstly, Baudrillard's comments on the death of the social do not mean exclusively that it is *sociology* which is in deep trouble. He is equally clear that it is the political which has suffered an abrupt and devastating termination. In historical terms, 'the political' arose in the Renaissance with Machiavelli's science of pure strategy, but the political has been finally subordinated, especially in Marxism, to the social. The triumph of the silent masses has coincided with the 'simultaneous decline' (Baudrillard 1983: 15) of the social and the political. Secondly, the problems of sociology cannot be easily separated from the historical rise and fall of Marxism. In the 1970s, structural Marxism promised to replace bourgeois, subjectivist sociology by a scientific Marxism which would constitute a real object of enquiry, namely, the mode of production. Max Weber, who was identified as the main protagonist of bourgeois values, was often the primary target of this attack on the credentials of sociology (Turner 1981). In the 1990s, the whole theoretical stance of intellectual Marxism has been made problematic as a consequence of the almost total failure of Marxist–Leninism as a political movement (Laclau 1990). As we will see, any interpretation of Baudrillard must take this radical transformation of Marxism into account, partly because Baudrillard's early work on the sociology of consumption evolved into a critique of existing Marxist theories of production, especially Marxist theories of value (Baudrillard 1975). Thirdly, the idea either that the founding fathers of sociology are under attack because they are too remote from the contemporary postmodern scene or that they, as the spokesmen of the grand narrative of Industrial Society, must be subjected to the critiques of deconstruction, feminism and postmodernism, is again not an exclusively disciplinary problem of sociology. Indeed one could plausibly argue that the whole issue in sociology is parasitic upon a more profound questioning of the classical high culture of Europe as *the* global grand narrative. Postmodernism as a 'theory' is bound up inevitably with the idea of decolonization, both in its geopolitical and cultural meanings. The challenge is thus very broad. It was after all in literary studies that the classical canon was challenged (and to some extent dissolved) by Marxism, feminism, cultural studies and finally postmodernism. Hence in many universities, literary studies have become cultural studies (Easthope 1991). These changes are also related to the long and complicated struggle over the implications of Paul de Man's deconstructive literary techniques for critical interpretation and hermeneutics.

The argument in this chapter takes the form of a modest defence of sociology against the idea of the death of the social in the postmodern epoch. This defence of sociology takes the following form. The overall strategy is to outflank postmodernism by showing that at least some aspects of postmodernist 'methodology' have been anticipated by earlier debates in anthropology and sociology around questions of interpretation, neutrality, subjectivity, meaning, and the textuality of meaning. However, unlike Callinicos, Kellner and other critics of Baudrillard, I take the stand that postmodernism does reflect important changes, not so much in the structure of industrial capitalism, but in the place and nature of culture. Baudrillard's celebration of the simulcra of modern society is an index of the loss of authority of high culture and its associated élites. The social sciences as a core feature of the academy, even at their most radical, are necessarily part of the national high culture, and thus an object of attack. Postmodernism thus brings into question the traditional status and historical role of the intellectual.

Firstly, in epistemological terms, we can take much of post-modernism, because it asks the question (what are the appropriate methods for studying modern social reality, especially a reality dominated by consumerism symbols?) as a modern version of the classical *Methodenstreit* which also wanted to know whether the methods of the natural science were relevant to the social, and indeed whether 'the social' could be studied at all. Weber's profound ambiguity about sociology and the social (terms which he character-istically always put in quotation marks) can be seen as a preview of the current debate. Secondly, the sense that the postmodern is a recent phenomenon needs to be tempered by a reinterpretation of the periodization of the modern and the postmodern. Postmodernism is not the first (and probably will not be the last) critique of the grand narrative of the modern. Thirdly, and related to this idea, a number of earlier debates in sociology, especially Daniel Bell's idea of post-industrial society (Bell 1973), had already anticipated the modern–postmodern contest. This commentary on the idea of post-industrial society suggests that there are substantively important historical continuities rather than a deep fissure in the social structure of capitalist society, but what has changed is the nature and place of culture. The weakness of traditional sociology has been its inability adequately to analyse culture. Postmodernism as a style of analysis can be seen as an attempt to provide an analysis of culture in late capitalism. The attraction of Baudrillard's work probably lies in its recognition of the failures of traditional social science frame-works for cultural analysis (especially the analysis of the production and consumption of signs). Finally, I want to suggest that we have to see Baudrillard's *America* and the related *Cool Memories* (Baudril-lard 1989 and 1990a) in the context of a particular tradition of American–European comparisons, which extends far beyond the most obvious comparisons with Alexis de Tocqueville's *Democracy in America* (1835). By attempting to show that these problems with the social (via Baudrillard and postmodernism) are not new but have followed the discipline of sociology throughout its existence, I suggest that, while sociological theory cannot be complacent, it need not feel surprised by the postmodern furore.

As a general rule, Baudrillard is widely regarded in sociology as the postmodernist *par excellence*. Chen (1987) refers to Baudrillard's theory as a case of 'implosive postmodernism'; Kellner (1989a and b) clearly identifies Baudrillard as part of the collapse of Marxism into postmodernism; and Lash (1990: 2) regards Baudrillard's work as 'an uncritical and even irresponsible celebration' of postmodernism. Certainly works like *America* and *Cool Memories* have many of the hallmarks of postmodernism: fragmented, ironic, reflexively parodying popular cultural forms, trivial and without form. *America* invites us to behave like the cool tourist – distant, alien, amoral, cruising. If Baudrillard's later works have the quality of a sociological fiction, they are quite unlike the 'serious' fiction of high modernity. It is perhaps useful to compare, in order to make a contrast, Baudrillard's *America* with the heavy Baroque style of Franz Kafka's unfinished *Amerika* (Kafka 1946). Kafka's novel explores the grand narratives of western literature, being a study of alienation, patriarchal authority, the Fall, and the Success Story, of which it is a parody (Murray 1991). It is at one level a satire on America as the Land of Opportunity, as the setting of the Horatio Alger story. Baudrillard's account of America, while also a reflection on the simulation of success, apparently avoids any 'serious' analysis. In this sense, Baudrillard's *America* appears to reflect the simulated opportunities of American culture by celebrating the trivia of social relations in late capitalism; it has the characteristics of celebratory postmodernism.

By contrast, Gane (1991a: 46) is one of the few writers to question the notion that Baudrillard is postmodern. Of course, Baudrillard himself tends to reject the label, and has been openly critical of the idea. It is probably more fruitful, following Gane (1991a: 32) and Plant (1992: 136), to treat Baudrillard's social analysis as a variant of the Situationist perspectives of Guy Debord (1987) in such publications as *Society of the Spectacle*. The modern world of advanced consumerism presents the workers with an endless spectacle of promises; commodities offer the promised land of eternal beauty and youthfulness. The society of consumer spectacle presents the workers with a world of abundance designed to satisfy their pseudo-needs. We can see Baudrillard's own fascination with commodity signs, advertising spectaculars, and the simulations of advanced capitalism as an extension of the Situationist vision of the workers' alienation, but Baudrillard's account of this world appears postmodern because, in accepting the irrelevance of criticism, it abandons any radical political project.

THE POSTMODERN FISSURE?

The fundamental sociological task is first to decide whether the major changes in the social structure and culture of modern societies suggest that we are now living in a postmodern society. Are the transformations of cultural and social life so profound that we have to conclude that we have crossed a historical fissure of the same magnitude as the transition from feudalism to capitalism? Alternatively, are these important changes merely an increase in the pace of modernity? Secondly, if these changes constitute a new society, as it were a postmodern mode of production, does it follow that the conceptual map of classical sociology no longer fits the postmodern terrain? Do we need not only a new map (a new language of the postmodern epoch) but a new school of cartographers to replace Marx, Weber and Durkheim? That is, is it time to forget social theory?

In his *The Consequences of Modernity*, Anthony Giddens (1990) has taken a clear and decisive stand on this issue. For Giddens, we are not moving into a postmodern society or epoch, but we are entering a period of radicalized or high modernity, which does pose a major discontinuity with earlier periods of modernity. He proposes a 'discontinuist' interpretation of modern history (Giddens 1990: 3), that is there is a fissure which thus separates radicalized, reflexive modernity from early modernity, and the discontinuist fissure has rendered much of classical sociology obsolete. Previous paradigms of classical sociology are thus inadequate because they suffer from evolutionism, from a failure to grasp the processes of globalization, and finally from an inability to understand the problems of modernist reflexivity. More specifically, existing sociological paradigms cannot conceptualize change because they adopt characteristically a unidimensional model of the causes of social change. Secondly, they tend to reify society which is equated with the nation state; such a conceptualization obscures globalizing, inter-civilizational processes. Finally, sociology has often seen itself as providing information which can give us control over social institutions. For Giddens, such a view of sociology is simplistic, because it fails to offer us a radical view of the reflexivity of modernity. A radicalized, reflexive modernity means that we have to understand the new opportunities and risks (Beck 1992) of a globalized world. This viewpoint permits Giddens to reject the idea that we have already moved into a postmodern epoch (Giddens 1990: 49–50), while retaining a claim which is analogous to postmodernism such that the characteristics of modern society have been superseded by a new set of social conditions. The fissure is there, but it invokes a division between modernity and radicalized modernity, not between modernity and postmodernity. To this new task of social analysis, classical sociology is redundant. We are invited not to forget classical social theory *tout court*, but to develop a reflexive social theory appropriate to high modernity.

Baudrillard also believes that there has been a radical fissure in the development of capitalist society. This historical collapse of a society based on the production of commodities and the arrival of a society based on the consumption of signs means that traditional theories, especially Marxism, are no longer relevant. Baudrillard has replaced the Marxist periodization of feudal, capitalist and communist transformations with the theory that there have been three distinctive epochs: primitive, heirarchical and mass societies. In primitive society, there is no element of signs. In hierarchical societies, a symbolic culture is developed and there is a limited circulation of signs. Finally, in mass society the circulation of signs becomes dominant. In a mass society, the media create an implosion where the sign no longer refers to the real. This is the epoch of hyperreality; the society of the mass. The mass cannot be analysed; it defies the penetration of social science concepts.

An alternative view, taken by Marxists like Alex Callinicos (1989) in *Against Postmodernism* is that nothing has changed. Capitalism as a socioeconomic system has not suffered any radical internal transformation, and the conventional Marxist categories are still relevant and still in place. Callinicos presents a defence of this argument partly by arguing against both Daniel Bell's post-industrialism thesis and Baudrillard's sociology of hyperreality. This is not necessarily the most appropriate place to offer a defence of Bell's sociology of post-industrialism (Liebowitz 1985; Turner 1989), but Callinicos's support for the continuity of Marxist thought because nothing has changed is extreme, given the political transformations of eastern Europe and the Soviet Union since his book was published. However, the technical criticisms of the post-industrialism thesis, for example with reference to the knowledge class, the development of the service sector, and the role of the university, are powerful.

A MODEST DEFENCE

How might one best respond to these three perspectives (Giddens, Baudrillard and Callinicos) of the historical fissure in the development of modern society? While we need to consider a number of specific issues within the sociology of late capitalism, it is important to realize that these theoretical responses have to be set within the political context of the demise of organized communism and the fragmentation of social movements such as feminism and the environmentalists. This context, as Chris Rojek notes in this study, is especially important in the case of Baudrillard.

The debate about postmodernism in social science cannot be separated from the current interest in globalization. Because the world as a system of societies is increasingly interconnected by new means of communication, trade, mobility and tourism, there is a much greater proximity and interaction between the world cultures. This development in itself has brought about an intensive form of eclecticism in culture. At the same time, the deregulation of markets, instability in trade, and the growth of world money markets have increased the risky nature of modern societies. Postmodernism can be regarded as a cultural system which corresponds to the disorganization and uncertainty of late capitalism. This perspective on the rise of postmodernity has been presented in a number of sociological works which have attempted to describe the disorganization of contemporary capitalism (Beck 1992; Lash and Urry 1987). However, while these developments are certainly very important, it is not clear that these characteristics of the contemporary global order are inherently different from the world system which emerged in the late sixteenth century and early seventeenth century with the global expansion of capitalism. Was the South Sea Bubble any less global or risky than the speculative capitalist activity of modern entrepreneurs like Alan Bond, Robert Maxwell, or Mr Holmes à Court? The idea that the entrepreneur has to operate in a climate of risk has been fundamental to economic and sociological theories of the global market throughout most of this century. The notion that uncertainty, instability and precariousness are somehow fundamental to the very organization of capitalism was expressed in the Marxist view that with capitalism 'all that is solid melts into air' (Berman 1983).

Many of the features of postmodern, global society were anticipated by Daniel Bell's analyses of post-industrial society. These post-industrial features include the explosion of knowledge, the dependence on the university as the power-house of further capitalist expansion, and the social impact of new information technology. Equally important, Bell's theory in his account of 'the public household' was based on the idea that capitalism is an unstable system. The rise of expectations in a mass democracy placed an unusual strain on the state, while also making great demands on the economy to produce sustained growth. Social Keynesianism combined with a revolution in consumer expectations created socioeconomic tensions which the state could not resolve in a democracy. Bell, of course, also produced a very interesting analysis of modern culture, because he argued that the decline of family capitalism was associated with an erosion of the old Protestant Ethic of asceticism and a corresponding development of hedonistic consumption.

While Bell's general theory has been much criticized, his analysis of the growing autonomy of culture has proved to be of critical importance. In fact it is within this niche – the analysis of culture and the understanding of the autonomy of the cultural – that the most important developments in modern social theory have taken place. However, because the sociology of culture has been rather slow to develop, postmodern theory and postmodern debate have dominated the analytical stage. It is for this reason that the neglect of Bell's cultural theory is particularly problematic.

Bell's essays on the public household and the contradictions of capitalism which were written between 1964 and 1972 were published as *The Coming of Post-Industrial Society* (1973) and *The Cultural Contradictions of Capitalism* (1976). They have proven to be an enormously influential albeit controversial diagnosis of late capitalism. Bell's theory is that late capitalism is subject to a number of major tensions, particularly between the various axial principles of the cultural, economic and political systems. We can state this theory briefly. First, Bell has argued that there is a major division between the economy and culture. Secondly, there is a major contradiction between the cultural system which gives an emphasis to hedonistic consumption and egoistic personal development, while the economy still requires asceticism, discipline, hard work and efficiency. The economy still operates in terms of values which are broadly derived from Weber's Protestant Ethic thesis. According to Bell, American culture is now dominated by a new sensibility, which is anti-institutional and antinomian. Its major exponents were Herbert Marcuse, Norman O. Brown and R. D. Laing. For Bell, the counter-cultural features of postmodernism actually had their roots in the 1920s with the transformation of credit, which, through the instalment plan, encouraged consumers not to defer gratification but to enjoy life now. The new ethic of pleasurable sensibility has brought about a profound disjunction between work and play, and production and consumption, which reflects an important historical transformation, namely the supremacy of the cultural sphere over economics. Thirdly, culture thus enjoys a new autonomy in post-industrial society, and operates largely independently from both politics and economics.

Bell's work anticipated much of the contemporary debate about postmodernism and the self. Bell's sociology was sensitive to the idea of the aestheticization of the self as pure subjectivity. The disappearance of the old constraints of labour, asceticism, saving and investing for future consumption, and Protestantism had liberated the modern self as a system of pleasure. The new Eupsychia was a post-industrial utopia of immediate gratification. In much of his analysis of modern culture, Bell provided a sociological framework for understanding postmodernism as a theory and postmodernity as a historical stage. I have dwelt on this issue in order to throw doubt firstly on the idea that the transition from post-industrialism to postmodernity is a sudden and fatal rupture, and secondly on the claim that all previous social theory is thereby redundant. Lyotard's significant dependence on Bell in *The Post-modern Condition* (1984) is an important indication of the continuities between 'conventional' or mainstream sociology and analyses of postmodernity. This dependence, in the case of Lyotard on Bell, has in fact often led to the accusation that Bell's alleged technological determinism (in particular that new information technology has transformed society) has found a perfect reflection in the technologism of much postmodern debate. While I do not accept this allegation of technologism in Bell's arguments, this commentary does indicate an additional continuity between earlier debates about communications and the mass media.

While, as far as one can tell, Baudrillard was not influenced by Bell's vision of the role of technology and the media in shaping post-industrialism, he was influenced by Marshall McLuhan's analysis (Gane 1991b: 48) of the impact of new media on the transformation of modern culture, especially in *The Gutenberg Galaxy* (McLuhan 1967). McLuhan was particularly sensitive to the idea that we live in a processed social world where human beings live in a complete technostructure. This technological environment is carried with us as extensions of our own bodies, but McLuhan did not adopt a pessimistic view of the age of anxiety, because his 'technological humanism' (Kroker *et al*. 1984) and Catholic values committed him to the idea of the immanence of reason and the hope of an escape from the labyrinth. Indeed, a global technological system could become the basis of a universalistic culture. Although he was fully aware of the sensory deprivation which he associated with the impact of the mass media, he none the less remained committed to the hope that these negative effects were not fatal. Baudrillard, who as we have noted was deeply influenced by McLuhan's idea that the content of messages was relatively unimportant in relation to their form, has embraced a very nihilistic position with respect to our processed environment.

Baudrillard's pessimistic view of the fissure in the historical development of the modern is based on his view of the masses. Baudrillard's analysis of the masses is a product of the Situationist responses to the May events of 1968, when it became increasingly obvious that the critical social movements of modern society would not be dominated by Marxist theory or directed by a vanguard of the working class. The crisis of May 1968 had not been predicted by Marxism or by mainstream sociology, but they did validate the claims of Situationists like Guy Debord in the journal *Internationale Situationiste*. However, if the crisis had been unanticipated by conventional political analysis, then the sudden collapse of the students' and workers' movements of 1968 found no easy explanation in the framework of mainstream social sciences. Baudrillard's concept of the inexplicable nature of the mass depend a great deal on the unusual circumstances surrounding the May events. By 1973 with the publication of *The Mirror of Production* (Baudrillard 1975), Baudrillard was already moving away from an orthodox Marxist view of production, arguing that Marxism, far from being an external critique of capitalism, was merely a reflection or mirror of the principal economistic values of capitalism. Instead of engaging in the production of meaning, a subversive, oppositional movement would have to challenge the system from the point of view of meaninglessness. Subversion would have to rob the social system of significance. In taking this stand, Baudrillard followed the Situationist claim that whatever can be represented can be controlled (Plant 1992: 137). The mass events of 1968 offered a promise of the nonrepresentational moment, the pure event of authenticity, which could not be explained, and therefore could not be manipulated. Baudrillard, in dismissing Marxist theory as a means of representing events, sought to replace the idea of a mode of production with a mode of disappearance.

In taking this attitude towards modern social movements, Baudrillard's argument also rests on the various meanings of the word 'mass'. Baudrillard is thus able to make allusions to the idea of physical substance, matter, the majority and the electrical meaning of earth. The translator's note to *In the Shadow of the Silent Majority* points out that *faire masse* can mean to form a majority and to form an earth. Baudrillard argues by allusion that the mass absorbs the electrical charges of social and political movements; the mass thus neutralizes the electrical charge of society. This use of allusion, parody and irony is typical of Baudrillard's mode of analysis, which is a type of sociological poetics, a style which is likely to make sociologists feel uncomfortable (Gane 1991a: 193). There is here also a continuity with the style of Dada and the Situationists. The poetic and striking character of Baudrillard's style has no counterpart in professional social science, least of all in the British context.

Baudrillard's 'sociological fictions' (1990a: 15) are striking and challenging, but they are not ultimately convincing. Arguments which depend on allusion, allegory and similar rhetorical devices are decorative but they are not necessarily powerful. The notion of 'mass society' already has a clearly worked out sociological critique. The idea of 'mass society' might have been relevant in describing the new markets which were created in the post-war period with the advent of innovative technologies, which had the immediate effect of lowering prices and making commodities available to a mass audience. However, the trend of sociological analysis in the last two decades has been to assert that mass audiences have been broken down into more selectively constructed niches for more individualized products. It is controversial to argue that industrialization necessarily produces a mass society, characterized by a common culture, uniform sentiments or an integrated outlook. The idea of a mass society was often associated with the notion that the decline of individualism would produce a directionless mass as the modern equivalent of the eighteenth-century mob. Critical theorists like Adorno and Marcuse associated the massification of society with authoritarianism and a potential for fascism. Of course,

Baudrillard's version of mass society is based on a particular view of the mass media creating a hyperreality in which the real has been absorbed by the hyperreal; meaning has imploded on itself. Although Baudrillard's analysis of hyperreality is post-critical (Chen 1987), he does adopt in practice a critical position towards American civilization, which is the extreme example of massification. Rather like critical theorists, Baudrillard believes that the (bourgeois) individual has been sucked into the negative electrical mass of the media age. However, sociological research on mass audiences shows that there is no ground for believing that media messages are received, consumed or used in any standardized manner, and the majority of social scientists working on culture have attempted to argue that cultural objects in the age of the mass media are appropriated, transformed and consumed in diverse forms and according to various practices (de Certeau 1984). In fact, sociologists, largely inspired by the Situationists, have argued that everyday life is resistant to massification and that the concrete reality of everyday life-situations is the principal arena within which opposition to massification can be expected. Everyday life was regarded by both Guy Debord and Henri Lefebvre (1991) as the foundation of authenticity. Baudrillard, by arguing that criticism belongs to the period of modernism and not to the age of hyperreality, has ruled out opposition to the system, at least at the level of public debate and formal politics.

To summarize this discussion, what sociological changes are associated with the idea that a radical transformation of modern society has occured? The features which are conceptualized as decisive in the postmodern fissure have been anticipated by many earlier sociological debates (about post-Fordism, disorganized capitalism, and post-industrialism), and there are strong reasons for seeing the contemporary development of a globalized risk society as merely an extension of the socioeconomic patterns of the world system.

I have argued elsewhere (Turner 1990) that many configurations of the postmodern world were present in the Baroque culture of the seventeenth century. Here was a culture which had been thrust into a global arena by European imperialism, which had a strong sense of the fragmented and constructed nature of the social, which developed an articulate notion of the anxiety and subjectivity of the self, and which practised parody and irony as rhetorical styles. The luxurious sensuality of Baroque public culture has been seen as a mixture of high, low and kitsch culture, which was designed to trap the masses in a simulated culture. If this reading of the Baroque is correct, then it makes the idea of a unique break in modernity in this century difficult to sustain. Instead we might see the Baroque period as a forerunner of the postmodern critique of modernity. From a sociological perspective, one can argue that modernity had its origins in the Protestant Reformation, the seventeenth-century development of agrarian capitalism, and in the colonial expansion of the world economic system. The opposition to this Protestant revolution was the Baroque culture of the absolutist period. Just as postmodernism is a critique of the metanarratives of modernism, so the Baroque was a critical movement against the metanarratives of Protestant modernism. This parallel between the Baroque and postmodernism suggests that the simplistic periodization of modernity/postmodernity should be abandoned.

CONCLUSION

These sociological and historical observations suggest that Baudrillard's account of the masses and simulation is, from a sociological point of view, less than convincing. Why then is Baudrillard important? The main argument to account for his influence must be situated within the general failure of conventional sociology to deal with the analysis of contemporary culture. Baudrillard's theory of consumption and the hyperreal society offers a perspective on culture which has been generally missing from traditional sociology and Marxism. The inability of Marxism and sociology to analyse culture opened up a space in modern social theory which has been occupied by postmodernism. The only exceptions to this argument are to be found in the work of writers like Georg Simmel, Walter Benjamin and more recently in the work of Daniel Bell. There are some interesting parallels between Baudrillard and Simmel, because Simmel appears to take a specific interest in the trivia of everyday life – ruins, style, Alpine journeys, clothing and so forth. Simmel often seems to have no distinctive political critique of modern society, apart from his critical *Philosophy of Money* (Simmel 1990), and he concentrated on the aesthetics of modern life (Frisby 1991).

Although a sociology of the specific character of culture in late capitalism is implicit in Benjamin, Simmel, Bell and others, the importance of Baudrillard for society lies in the fact that he has attempted to address the peculiar features of postmodern culture in contemporary society, and he has developed a unique style for its analysis. Classical sociology had no satisfactory perspective on culture, and much recent debate has continued to be dominated by an outmoded Marxism (Turner 1992). Baudrillard has been noticeably successful in capturing the fragmented, ironic, constructed, simulated features of mass culture, and he has accurately perceived the erosion of the authority of high culture in an age of advanced electronic technology. Baudrillard's own style especially in *America* and *Cool Memories* is successful because it simulates the condition it wishes to convey rather than producing a critical style in opposition to postmodern culture. It is this simulated effect of Baudrillard's poetics which has been a source of offence within the academy.

REFERENCES

Adorno, T. (1991) *The Culture Industry*, London, Routledge.
Bauman, Z. (1992) *Intimations of Postmodernity*, London, Routledge.
Baudrillard, J. (1975) *The Mirror of Production*, St. Louis, Telos Press.
—— (1983) *In the Shadow of the Silent Majorities*, New York, Semiotext(e).
—— (1989) *America*, London, Verso.
—— (1990a) *Cool Memories*, London, Verso.
—— (1990b) *Revenge of the Crystal*, London, Pluto.
Beck, U. (1992) *Risk Society*, London, Sage.
Bell, D. (1973) *The Coming of Post-Industrial Society*, New York, Basic Books.
—— (1976) *The Cultural Contradictions of Capitalism*, New York, Basic Books.
Berman, M. (1983) *All That is Solid Melts into Air*, London, Verso.
Callinicos, A. (1989) *Against Postmodernism, a Marxist Critique*, Cambridge, Polity Press.
Certeau, M. de (1984) *The Practice of Everyday Life*, Berkeley, University of California Press.
Chen, K.-H. (1987) 'The masses and the media: Baudrillard's implosive postmodernism', *Theory, Culture and Society* 4(1), 71–88.
Debord, G. (1987) *The Society of the Spectacle*, London, Rebel Press.
Denzin, N. K. (1991) *Images of Postmodern Society. Social Theory and Contemporary Cinema*, London, Sage.
Durkheim, E. (1992) *Professional Ethics and Civic Morals*, London, Routledge.
Easthope, A. (1991) *Literary into Cultural Studies*, London, Routledge.
Featherstone, M. (ed.) (1988) *Postmodernism*, London, Sage.
—— (1991) *Consumer Culture and Postmodernism*, London, Sage.

Frisby, D. (1991) 'The aesthetics of modern life: Simmel's interpretation', *Theory, Culture and Society* 8(3), 73–93.

Game, A. (1991) *Undoing the Social. Towards a Deconstructive Sociology*, Milton Keynes, The Open University Press.

Gane, M. (1991a) *Baudrillard. Critical and Fatal Theory*, London, Routledge.

—— (1991b) *Baudrillard's Bestiary. Baudrillard and Culture*, London, Routledge.

Giddens, A. (1990) *The Consequences of Modernity*, Cambridge, Polity Press.

Habermas, J. (1987) *The Philosophical Discourse of Modernity*, Cambridge, Polity Press.

Haraway, D. J. (1991) *Simians, Cyborgs and Women. The Reinvention of Nature*, London, Free Association Books.

Hollander, P. (1992) *Anti-Americanism. Critiques at Home and Abroad 1965–1990*, Oxford, Oxford University Press.

Jameson, F. (1984) 'Postmodernism or the logic of late capitalism', *New Left Review* 146, 53–92.

—— (1985) 'Postmodernism and consumer society', pp. 111–25 in Hal Foster (ed.) *Postmodern Culture*, London and Sydney, Pluto Press.

Jencks, C. (1977) *The Language of Post-Modern Architecture*, New York, Rizzoli.

Kafka, F. (1946) *Amerika*, New York, New Directions.

Kellner, D. (1989a) *Jean Baudrillard. From Marxism to Postmodernism and Beyond*, Cambridge, Polity Press.

—— (1989b) 'Boundaries and borderlines: reflections on Jean Baudrillard and critical theory', *Current Perspectives in Social Theory* 9, 5–22.

Kroker, A., Kroker, M-L. and Cook, D. (1984) *Panic Encyclopedia*, London, Macmillan.

Laclau, E. (1990) *New Reflections on the Revolution of Our Time*, London, Verso.

Lash, S. (1990) *Sociology of Postmodernism*, London, Routledge.

Lash, S. and Urry, J. (1987) *The End of Organized Capitalism*, Cambridge, Polity Press.

Lefebvre, H. (1991) *Critique of Everyday Life*, London, Verso.

Lefort, C. (1988) *Democracy and Political Theory*, Cambridge, Polity Press.

Liebowitz, N. (1985) *Daniel Bell and the Agony of Modern Liberalism*, Westport, Connecticut, Greenwood Press.

Lyotard, J.-F. (1984) *The Postmodern Condition. A Report on Knowledge*, Manchester, University of Manchester Press.

McLuhan, M. (1967) *The Gutenberg Galaxy*, London, Routledge & Kegan Paul.

Murray, J. (1991) *The Landscapes of Alienation. Ideological Subversion in Kafka, Celine and Onetti*, Stanford, University of Stanford Press.

Nicholson, L. J. (ed.) (1990) *Feminism/Postmodernism*, New York and London, Routledge.

Offe, C. (1985) *Disorganized Capitalism*, Cambridge, Polity Press.

Plant, S. (1992) *The Most Radical Gesture. The Situationist International in a Postmodern Age*, London, Routledge.

Robertson, R. (1990) 'Mapping the global condition: globalization as the central concept', pp. 15–31 in M. Featherstone (ed.) *Global Culture*, London, Sage.

Simmel, G. (1990) *The Philosophy of Money*, London, Routledge.

Smart, B. (1992) *Modern Conditions, Postmodern Controversies*, London, Routledge.

Stauth, G. and Turner, B. S. (1988) *Nietzsche's Dance. Resentment, Reciprocity and Resistance in Social Life*, Oxford, Basil Blackwell.

Turner, B. S. (1981) *For Weber. Essays in the Sociology of Fate*, London, Routledge & Kegan Paul.

—— (1989) 'From postindustrial society to postmodern politics: the political sociology of Daniel Bell', pp. 199–217 in J. Gibbins (ed.) *Contemporary Political Culture*, London, Sage.

—— (ed.) (1990) *Theories of Modernity and Postmodernity*, London, Sage.

—— (1991) 'Politics and culture in Islamic globalism', pp. 161–82 in R. Robertson and W. R. Garrett (eds) *Religion and Global Order*, New York, Paragon House.

—— (1992) 'Ideology and utopia in the formation of an intelligentsia: reflections on the English cultural conduit', *Theory, Culture and Society* 9(1), 183–210.

Vidich, A. J. (1991) 'Baudrillard's *America*', *Theory, Culture and Society* 8(2), 135–44.

Weber, M. (1965) *The Protestant Ethic and the Spirit of Capitalism*, London, Allen & Unwin.

Chapter 5

Baudrillard's woman
The Eve of seduction

Sadie Plant

The death of the subject has made a good postmodernist slogan. The obituaries have been written, and the legacies distributed. But its end, so far, has been merely symbolic, and for all the shifts and confusions of postmodernity, the subject remains the basic and superior unit of even the most deconstructed world. Fragmented and decentred, the postmodern subject is merely a new and improved version of its modernist self; an updated model no longer vulnerable to the dissolution it once feared; a subject even rejuvenated by its pretended dissolution. It has learnt to live with the challenge of shifting foundations and uncertain perimeters and become reconciled with the vulnerability of its identity. The subject has neither collapsed into the object nor disappeared into circuits of image and sign; seduced and abandoned, it has nevertheless reconciled itself with the vulnerability of identity and today stands as certain and assured of its lack of self as its earlier model was of itself. The obituaries were premature.

Nevertheless, the subject continues to be haunted by its death. This is beyond question even for Baudrillard, who knows that identity is possible only in relation to that which lies beyond it: dissolution, nothing, the void, the meaningless. This is the forbidden zone outside every human domain, and marks the absolute limit beyond which all that is life, production, doing and making is lost. It is the zone most feared, but also that which is most desired: 'If you were to see written on a door panel: "This opens onto the void" ', asks Baudrillard, 'wouldn't you still want to open it?' (Baudrillard 1990a: 75). Of course one would always be tempted: to open the door is to lose oneself, a fatal loss which is none the less craved and is, moreover, essential to the existence of the subject. The encounter with the door provides the subject with a backdrop of dissolution against which it can measure its own identity. It places the subject in no danger as long as the question is hypothetical: 'wouldn't you . . . want to open it?'. This is Baudrillard's strategy in *Seduction*: to face the door, and in so doing ensure that its closure is never in question. The subject needs to be threatened: while it is vulnerable, it knows who it is. The threat must seem credible and appear to pose a real danger, but this is all it must do: seem and appear. It must be a threat minimal and contained, the image of danger rather than danger itself. The trick is to see the door, but refuse that which lies beyond it. A strategy which protects the subject from the question of dissolution and pays homage to the void in order to keep the subject on the safe side of nothingness. The void is the great fear, too great to be ignored, but too fearful to admit. Baudrillard renders it credible and conceivable, known and meaningful; he writes of nothingness in order to avoid death. Still haunted by its end, the postmodern subject can now know death as a symbolic game in which it lets itself play, paddling in the shallows of dissolution and always facing the shore.

These shallows are seduction, the 'superficial abysses' of a void become mapped and defined, the image of nothing. Seduction is only appearance; not the void which lies behind it, for there is nothing there. Only the simulacra of nothing is possible, only the simulation of the void. There is no longer something and nothing, nor a possible passage from one to the other. Both the real and the void are counterfeit in their pretensions to reality and nothingness. Appearance is the real operation of both; the moment before the void is the entire operation of the world, the perpetual motion of postmodernity. Seduction stands between something and nothing; with 'neither substance nor origin' (p. 82), it is neither 'simple appearance, nor a pure absence, but the eclipse of presence' (p. 85).

Seduction is more than the identification of a new force of production in the world, just as appearance is in more than a diametrical relation to the real. Not even merely the unproductive, it is that which 'is never "produced", is never found where it is produced' (pp. 7–8) and as such forever eludes the discourse of production and undermines the very idea that there is a real world and that something, be it the proletariat, capital, desire, or discourse, makes it go round. The culture of the modern, industrial subject 'produces everything, makes everything speak, everything babble, everything climax' (p. 20); in a world which 'wanted us to believe that . . . the play of productive forces is what regulates the course of things' (p. 84). At the heart of the world as viewed by Marx, Freud, Nietzsche, production remains the paradigm for those who have more recently developed their work: Foucault, for whom power is the productive force; Deleuze and Guattari, for whom desire is the machinic energy; Irigaray, for whom woman is the source. These are writers whom Baudrillard's seduction traps within an old productivist ethos, where their discourses of power and liberation merely reinforce the narratives which insist that truths must be revealed, secrets unveiled, desires emancipated and subjectivities made and remade. The liberation they seek can only be subjection to the orders of production, the power they invoke is the *'mastery of the real universe'* (p. 8), the realm of that which is productive and produced. To all this, Baudrillard's question is: 'what if everything, contrary to appearances – in fact, in accord with a secret rule of appearances – operates by seduction?' (pp. 83–4). What if the real universe, in which everything is freed, revealed, and made to happen, is merely a pretence, the superficial surface of the superficial abysses which are the operation of the real?

This move gives Baudrillard's discourse the appearance of a radicalism which eclipses even the most radical of postmodern discourses. But perhaps even this is chimerical: riddled with hidden agendas and counterfeit claims, Baudrillard's work is really an attempt to protect the subject, not against seduction, for seduction is no threat at all, but against what he can only think as the void, the threat of dissolution. Indeed, just as he invokes the door in order to protect himself from the void which lies behind it, so Baudrillard looks to seduction to provide a barrier between nothing and something, death and the subject. Seduction becomes the guarantor: as long as seduction is possible, there must be a subject to be seduced. And this subject is masculine, as Baudrillard is quick to admit and happy to assume, while that which seduces is its 'missing dimension' (p. 67), the feminine.

While Baudrillard does not intend this conflation of the seductive and the feminine to make seduction the sole prerogative of women, it is they who have *'mastery over the symbolic universe'* (p. 8) and all that extends beyond the meanings and desires of the real and masculine world: the universe of the firm and the definite, sex and certainty, power and intention. Whatever seeks liberation wants to enter this realm of the sure and upstanding; to destroy the ambiguities and mysteries which themselves constitute the real and hidden order of things and subject every fluidity to the masculine orders of production. What it seeks to destroy is seduction, the hidden operation of the 'symbolic universe' which underwrites the world of men and things. Liberation, particularly women's liberation, is trapped in 'a strange, fierce complicity' with the masculine 'order of truth' (p. 8); hopelessly caught within a discourse of production which can only destroy the real object of its emancipation.

In feminism Baudrillard sees only the destruction of woman, a denial of the feminine, a rejection of seduction in favour of mis-guided demands for participation within the orders of production. Liberation is the discourse of an enlightenment humanism which wants to 'liberate the servile sex . . . in the very terms of its servitude' (p. 17), a misguided struggle for freedom whose only consequence can be to subsume woman within the parameters of a barely changed and hostile order. When woman demands, desires, and liberates herself, she abandons the seductive mode which is her own and only strength and enters into a culture for which liberation is a way of life and not at all a threatening demand. She accepts the terms which would eradicate every zone of secrecy, mystery, and artifice; she comes to live in a world where everything is forced to declare itself, open itself up, reveal its truth, express its desire, and search for its meaning. She escapes from the shadows only to find herself in the cruel light of an order for which everything must be measured and identified; too late she realizes that the autonomy, truth and desire she has won are really the very instruments of her oppression.

Feminism signals the end of uncertainty, a world for which there are 'no more secrets', the beginning of a 'radical obscenity' (p. 20) which wants everything out in the open. It is a process by which femininity is normalized and brought within the masculine:

> Femininity in this sense is on the same side as madness. It is because madness secretly prevails that it must be normalized (thanks to, amongst other things, the hypothesis of the uncon-scious). It is because femininity secretly prevails that it must be recycled and normalized (in sexual liberation in particular).
>
> (Baudrillard 1990a: 17)

Woman's insistence that she too must have meaning and purpose, desires and discourses of her own is a misguided rejection of her own and only powers. These are the powers of the secret and the artificial, that which is undecidable and manifest in ritual, game, ceremony, and seduction.

Yes, women have been dispossessed of their bodies, their desires, happiness and rights. But they have always remained mistresses of this possibility of eclipse, of seductive disappearance and translucence, and so have always been capable of eclipsing the power of their masters.

(p. 88)

Eclipse has nothing to do with struggle, emancipation, or any of the discourses of power, of course. Women eclipse power; they do not enter into it, but exist with merely 'the flickering of a presence' (p. 85). For Baudrillard, this is the never quite real world of seduction, an effect of nothing, but itself the secret government of the real world of men and things. Woman is 'but appearance', but as such she 'thwarts masculine depth' (p. 10) and bears 'the immense privilege' of the feminine: 'the privilege of never having acceded to truth or meaning' (p. 8). This is the privilege of that which appears and disappears in blissful ignorance of the meanings and significance, the manifestations and satisfaction demanded by the productive. Far beyond production but always immanent to it, seduction is what makes the productive vulnerable to its own truth, and this truth is itself the deceit of seduction.

This is the privilege which woman, with feminism, wants to toss aside in favour of a subjectivity, a sexuality, desires and meanings of her own. Woman wants to become real, and this, for Baudrillard, is her big mistake.

What does the women's movement oppose to the phallocratic structure? Autonomy, difference, a specificity of desire and pleasure, a different relation to the female body, a speech, a writing – but never seduction . . . They do not understand that seduction represents mastery over the symbolic universe, while power represents only the mastery of the real universe.

(p. 8)

(Master of the symbolic universe? Is this like being a king of the kitchen, the unseen hand that rocks the [preferably] unseen cradle?) Why, he asks, is there a continual attempt to find equivalence and opposition to the masculine? Bodies, pleasures, writings and politics: why challenge the masculine with feminine equivalents, when this is a strategy which already accepts the 'essentially masculine' (p. 7) opposition between the masculine and the feminine? The search for a female sexuality, no matter how plural, multiple, and fluid it might be, remains trapped within this phallic separation, and seduction is the term which takes us beyond the old, productive polarity and 'breaks the distinctive sexualization of bodies and the inevitable phallic economy that results' (p. 10). The masculine has no opposite, no rival, there is no sex but the male: 'Freud was right: there is but one sexuality, one libido – and it is masculine . . . There is no use dreaming of some non-phallic, unlocked, unmarked sexuality' (p. 6). Female sexuality is a contradiction in terms, a productive seduction, an impossibility. The subject can only be masculine, and man is the only subject. Everything else is the object of his desire, the seductive, beyond the phallic but irrevocably exterior to the real universe. Seduction cannot exist in the world of men and things; occult and mysterious, it is the enigmatic, the insoluble and must remain so if it is to remain at all.

Without desire and stealing its pleasures from games of entrapment and challenge, strategy and artifice, it thinks nothing of the natural, the authentic or the real, and cares only for the thrill of the chase, a game it plays by rules entirely of its own. It is image, appearance, the very process of appearance and disappearance, reversibility and pretence. Seduction is 'not a matter of believing, doing, wanting, or knowing' (p. 76). It knows no meaning and eludes all discourse; it wants only to play in a world of schemes and enchantments, enticement and ruse; its operations have no goal and seek no object. It is the insubstantial underside of the orders of meaning and power inhabited by the desiring, masculine subject. It reverses the real and implodes the meaningful; it tempts the world of men and things into lies and confusion, illusion and dissolution; it is the magic of glamour, the spell of the counterfeit, the diabolical. And in all this it stands in a secret and powerful relation to the world of men and things, a threat which 'continues to haunt them from without, and from deep within its forsaken state, threatening them with collapse' (p. 2).

Woman's secret is that she is never quite real, never quite true, never 'a signified desire, but the beauty of an artifice' (p. 76). She exists only as this ambiguity: 'everything that is no longer ambiguous is masculine in kind' (Baudrillard 1990b: 80) and all that is feminine 'incarnates reversibility, the possibility of play and symbolic involvement' (1990a: 21). The feminine is 'something that is nothing' (p. 7), neither something nor nothing, 'neither a marked nor an unmarked term. It does not mark the "autonomy" of desire,

pleasure, or the body, or of a speech or writing that it has supposedly lost(?). Nor does it lay claim to some truth of its own. It
seduces' (p. 7). If it was ever possible to speak of woman's sexuality,
this was it: she wanted nothing and had no desire: she seduced.
Before the intervention of feminism's 'beautiful souls who, retro-
spectively, see woman as alienated from time immemorial, and then
liberated' (p. 19), this was the role within which woman was
'entirely herself, she was in no way defeated, nor passive, nor did
she dream of her future "liberation" ' (p. 19).

Irigaray's invocations of a woman's writing and a female sexuality are taken as a the epitome of an attempt to drag woman into the
orders of discourse and the real. Baudrillard quotes a passage from
'This sex which is not one', and condemns Irigaray for what he
takes as her celebrations of sexual difference and the pleasures of
woman. And yet Baudrillard knows that Irigaray's entire project is
to escape the very 'phallic economy' he identifies: *Seduction* is
written with close reference to her work, and it is not merely the
disparaged discourse of female sexuality that he takes from her
writing. For Irigaray's woman is absent too, without desire, bereft
of power, and so the locus of mystery and ambiguity. 'Not knowing
what she wants', woman is always 'ready for anything' (Irigaray
1981: 100), she 'does not have a sex', and is entirely beyond the
singular and the certain. Even plurality is too contained, for
woman 'experiences pleasure almost everywhere' and her sexuality
cannot be named, cannot exist in the world of men and things.
' "She" is indefinitely other in herself' (p. 103), she is 'neither one
nor two' (p. 101), and it is this indeterminacy which accounts for
'the mystery that she represents in a culture that claims to enumer-
ate everything, cipher everything by units, inventory everything by
individualities' (p. 101).

There is no demand for equality or equivalence in Irigaray's
writing; and Baudrillard knows that she too wants nothing to do
with struggles for power and the entry of woman into the existing
economy: 'In this race for power, woman loses the uniqueness of
her pleasure' (p. 104). Irigaray's woman is the 'nothing to be seen',
her cunt 'offers nothing to the view' and 'has no distinctive form of
its own'; indeed her pleasure is 'precisely in this incompleteness of
the form of her sex organ, which is why it retouches itself indefinitely' (p. 101). Baudrillard responds with derision to Irigaray's
'anatomical speech', and with seduction claims to move beyond the
terms of anatomical difference. The feminine is not a sex,

. . . but what counters the sex that alone has full rights and the full exercise of these rights, the sex that holds a monopoly on sex: the masculine, itself haunted by the fear of something other, of which sex is the disenchanted form: seduction . . . It is these two fundamental forms that confront each other in the male and female, and not some biological difference or some naive rivalry of power.

(Baudrillard 1990a: 21)

Nevertheless, it is clear that seduction and production are the terms of an equally anatomical discourse. Irigaray evokes 'a few of the specifically female pleasures' (p. 103), but these merely serve to indicate the impossibility of female sexuality within Baudrillard's phallic economy. If seduction goes beyond anatomy, it too is only by becoming the 'something that is nothing', the hidden and unnameable, and so returning to the Freudian gesture which has woman as the 'nothing to be seen'. The mystery and enigma of woman is the strange void of her sex, while the 'masculine is not made for ambiguity, it only exists in erection' (Baudrillard 1990b: 80).

While Baudrillard condemns what he sees as the feminist attempt to make everything speak, to destroy seduction and open up the secret of the hidden operation of the world, he also insists that seduction is always and irrevocably invulnerable and can never be undermined by the orders of production. Seduction always escapes the powers of the masculine; it is always elsewhere, never where the subject thinks it is. The goals of production are endlessly deferred; the horizons of liberation continually receded. The masters of the real universe are always under threat, for 'nothing is greater than seduction, not even the order that destroys it' (p. 2). And yet Baudrillard's attack on feminism would seem to suggest that seduction is indeed vulnerable to the orders of production and the discourse of liberation. So what is to be feared from a feminism which, as Baudrillard characterizes it, is doomed to defeat and repetition?

Something else, implicit yet concealed in seduction, is seen to threaten it; not production, but another tendency to which it is vulnerable and from which it must be preserved. For if seduction is indeed 'sovereign' and 'prevails, secretly, over the dominant form' (p. 17), the realm of the real, the productive, poses no threat. A sovereign seduction is never threatened by the real world of men

and things, but is only more or less threatening to it. And once it
has been unleashed as the sovereign and secret operation of the
world, it is uncontainable; there is nothing which can control it,
nothing to prevent it from becoming more threatening. Seduction
may be delightful in its lack of purpose, desire, and meaning, but
its attractions may also be fatal; it may tempt and excite, challenge
and deceive, but it also yawns as the terrible abyss over which the
real is suspended, a vertiginous crevice which pulls at the world of
men and things. Seduction is a slippery term, too ambiguous to be
confined, too powerful to be contained; it has no need of Baudrillard's protection, and is in any case beyond his jurisdiction. But
while Baudrillard knows that 'the attraction of the void lies at the
basis of seduction' (p. 77), he intends seduction to be only the
appearance of the void, merely its sign, a door which is never
opened. Seduction becomes the border, the limit, beyond which
there is nothing; the measure against which the masculine subject
can be certain of itself. Indeed, this is a seduction which guarantees
the subject, the moment just before the void, the border which can
safely be occupied, the 'sacred horizon of appearances' which pre-
serves the subject from death. It is only the dreams of losing
control and the collapse of meaning which tempt and seduce, not
the possibility that they might come true. Seduction is only the
promise of seduction, a flirtation with dissolution. The void
remains a black hole, but seduction makes the fall impossible: 'at
the edge of this black hole the point of no return becomes a point of
total reversibility, a catastrophic point where death is to be pulled
tight in a new seduction effect' (p. 128). Death as merely a new
effect: the void is avoided, the subject pulls through. There is no
outside, it was only a dream, the nightmare of modernist man.
There's nothing out there, scrabbling at the door; there's nothing
on the other side. The outside is merely the mirror of the inside, the
screen on which man projects himself, the backdrop against which
he acts in the world. The feminine, the object of desire, the
counterfeits and appearances of the world: 'What are they, and
what do they do behind this screen? They make themselves into an
impenetrable and unintelligible surface, which is a way of fading';
they 'eclipse themselves, they melt into the shallow screen'
(Baudrillard 1990c: 86). Everything is on the interior, the void is
become a screen, nothing but the play of signs, the comings and
goings of meaning, the secret games played out in the world.
    Indeed it is by virtue of its games and rituals that seduction

remains poised on the brink of the black hole. Outside the laws of production, nature, and meaning, seduction has nothing to do with the chaos of anarchy but is more akin to a different form of government. 'Seduction supposes a ritual order, sex and desire a natural order' (1990a: 21). Whereas 'sex is a function', seduction 'is a game', a process of rule and rite, ceremony and artifice; neither 'an inversion nor subversion of the law, but its reversion in simulation' (p. 149). Seduction is not meaningful, but neither is it entirely without meaning: it is 'the sensual and intelligible form of non-sense' (p. 70), a meaningful meaninglessness, a void which can be known, 'an enigmatic state which is neither life nor death' (1990b: 24). Seduction has nothing to do with chance, or the total liberty of the indeterminate. It is cyclical, a matter of convention and recurrence, an arbitrary sequence but a sequence none the less. 'The Rule plays on an immanent sequence of arbitrary signs, while the law is based on a transcendent sequence of necessary signs' (1990a: 133). The law cannot be transgressed; meaning is escaped only 'by replacing it with a more radical simulacrum, a still more conventional order' (1990a: 138).

This seduction is merely a game. It is aristocratic, with duels and challenges, courtships and ceremonies, a mode in which the subject can indulge; a seduction which merely wants to play with the subject and will tempt him with dissolution but never entirely destroy him. In its aristocratic form, seduction promises a fantasy which secures man's mastery of the real universe. But the game can never be real: seduction is only a way of playing with the pieces of the real world. If the game becomes serious, seduction does indeed begin to dissolve the certainties of the masculine.

Baudrillard's task, then, is to protect seduction from its own worst excesses, and in so doing protect the masculine subject from the point at which seduction becomes more than a game. That this is the real task of his writings on seduction is particularly clear in the closing sections of *Seduction*, where Baudrillard finally abandons the pretence that seduction is threatened by the real and confirms that there are forms of seduction which must be resisted, versions which take themselves to an extreme at which the subject, rather than the seductive, is in danger. Indeed, he suggests that seduction is already exceeding the rules, refusing to play the game to the advantage of man. It is not merely feminism that threatens the aristocratic seduction necessary to the survival of the subject, but also the screens, formulae, and bits of the information age.

When Baudrillard turns his attentions to the digitalized, virtual worlds of advanced capitalism, he sees cool and lifeless tendencies creeping across the real world of men and things. The seductions of the postmodern age have no respect for the ritual, the game, the strategy; they are inhuman, alien, threatening to the subject, they introduce us to 'an age of soft technologies, of genetic and mental software' (1990a: 172), soft drugs and cool electronics, in which man can no longer be certain and firm.

Seduction becomes cool at the moment in which it refuses to be man's mirror, the backdrop, the scene against which he acts in the world. As Baudrillard knows, 'the old structures of knowledge, the concept, the scene, the mirror, attempt to create illusion and thus they emphasise a truthful projection of the world' (1990c: 87), but the possibility that these theatrical arenas might disappear is beyond the tolerance even of the new, seduceable postmodern subject. The mirror is essential as the boundary which stands between man and what he fears as the void, a limit which shines back to the subject and gives him the reflection by which he knows himself.

In the information age, the mirror is indeed threatened; the digital is said to give the secret operations of seduction an unprecedented exposure. As is the case with his attacks on feminism, however, Baudrillard's primary concern is not with the triumph of the productive but the collapse of a seduction on which man can rely and in relation to which he can be sure of himself. The point at which the seductive enters into the world is not the death of seduction, but the death of the subject; and in the postmodern world this death is heralded less by the entry of seduction into the real, than by the collapse of the subject into seduction itself. With the digital technologies of the information age, the temptations faced by man are no longer those of an aristocratic and ceremonial seduction, but the cool and complex excesses of a seduction which begins to point beyond itself and open the door which leads onto the void. This is the point at which seduction no longer operates as a mirror, or limit for man, the moment in which the game is no longer played to his benefit but instead begins to absorb him in alien networks amongst which he can find no meaning. There is no challenge in this 'playful eroticization of a world without stakes' (1990a: 156). Beyond even 'the sensual and intelligible forms of non-sense', cool seduction is the 'debasement of play to the level of function' (p. 158), the collapse of the rules, 'the cybernetic absorption of play into the general category of the ludic' (p. 159). Here the subject is no longer sure of himself, suddenly vulnerable to temptations which threaten his very identity.

> Without too much effort, one sees the world of psychotropic drugs: for the latter too is ludic, being nothing but the manipulation of a sensorial keyboard or neuronic instrument panel. Electronic games are a soft drug – one plays with them with the same somnambular and tactile euphoria.
>
> (1990a: 159)

Tossed into 'this light, psychedelic giddiness which results from multiple or successive connections and disconnections', the digital age invites us 'to become miniaturized "game systems"', i.e. microsystems with the potential to regulate their own random functioning' (p. 162).

Characteristic of the information age, the ludic is a mode in which everything still 'moves around, and can give the impression of an operative seduction' (p. 163) but has little to do with the aristocratic reality of its games. No longer the seduction of ritual and game, information technology brings us into a world in which the subject is merely a point on the network, a terminal in a cyber-spatial zone. The games continue to be played, but they are no longer games he understands; the rules are incomprehensible, the strategies make no sense to him, the meaning disappears. The '0/1 of binary or digital systems is no longer a distinctive opposition or established difference. It is a "bit", the smallest unit of electronic impulse – *no longer a unit of meaning* . . . This is what the matrix of information and communication is like, and how the networks function' (p. 165). Here the death of the subject becomes possible at last: 'Two terminals do not two interlocutors make. In "tele" space . . . there are no longer any *determinate terms* or positions. Only *terminals* in a position of *ex-termination*' (p. 165).

After long detours through imagined threats and dreamed dangers, man finally confronts his death at the computer terminal. But Baudrillard clings onto the conviction that this is not the dissolution of an ultimate seduction, but a death caused by overdosing on the real. The screen, he insists, is not the manifestation of an alien operation, but merely the repetition of the same, an image too ideal, a projection too perfect to serve as a measure for man.

For Baudrillard, information technology threatens the difference on which man depends only because it engages the masculine subject in an endless and pointless circuit of self-referentiality. The mirror is destroyed only because man abandons it in an attempt to replicate himself, a process of self-seduction in which he begins to sink into his own image. Baudrillard sees this process epitomized in the robot and the clone, accused of destroying seduction by pretending to equivalence with man, bringing what should remain secret into the light. While such pretenders are 'but appearance', they exist only to the benefit of man, but in any excess of this role they become hostile and threatening. The automaton, epitomized by the early clockwork toy, is merely an artificial man which poses no threat to his standing: indeed, it is intriguing and seductive precisely because of the distance which remains between man and machine. Counterfeit and artificial, it is 'an interrogation upon nature, the mystery of the existence or nonexistence of the soul, the dilemma of appearance and being. It is like God: what's underneath it all, what's inside, what's in the back of it?'. Man needs mystery as 'his interlocutor', and only 'the counterfeit men [automata] allow these problems to be posed' (1988: 68). With the robot, however, we leave the seductive, and 'enter (re)production . . . the realm of the mercantile law of value and its calculations of force' (p. 72). As feminism would rob woman of her mystery, so the robot would rob the machine of its own enigma and artifice. And likewise the clone, the other become real and so useless to man, which Baudrillard warns is the endless reproduction of the same, the destruction of difference and ambiguity, the beginnings of a narcissism 'whose source is no longer a mirror but a formula' (1990a: 168), a formula with which man will reproduce and so destroy himself, for 'the subject's intimacy with himself rests on the immateriality of his double, on the fact that it is and remains a phantasy' (p. 168).

But is the screen the reproduction of man, the triumph of the orders of production, the survival of the phallic economy? Is information technology a process by which the image becomes real and so loses its mystery? While Baudrillard claims that the 'mirror phase has given way to the video phase', an 'effect of frantic self-referentiality, a short-circuit which immediately hooks up like with like' (Baudrillard 1988: 36–7), the information age does not destroy difference and mystery but, on the contrary, collapses man into the screen and plunges him into a world whose mystery has no meaning, not even the function of seduction. This is the point at which 'one can no longer speak of a sphere of enchantment or seduction' (1990a: 158); the point at which man is bereft of even his

I've seen enough TV
I know what happens

most superficial horizons, even the horizon of appearances sacred to him. Seduction becomes real, and the danger in this lies not at all in the danger that it is absorbed within the orders of production but, on the contrary, that man is absorbed, this time definitively, within the orders of a cold seduction which reaches beyond itself to the terrible dread of a death become real. Man is without hope if the play becomes real, if the backdrop disappears, if woman becomes real, the game begins to play itself, if the machine refuses to be man's interlocuter. These are the points at which all strategies depart from meaning: 'Contact for contact's sake becomes the empty form with which language seduces itself when it no longer has anything to say' (p. 164), and all that is left is the vertigo of a deathly fascination, a terminal seduction which will not let the subject live but will drag him into the black hole forever. We 'are living off seduction, but will die in fascination' (p. 157), for the subject 'presupposes a mirror, the mirror in which the subject alienates himself in order to find himself', and 'here there is no mirror' (p. 169). Cool seduction finds the subject 'living in a supple, curved universe, that no longer has any vanishing points' (p. 157). This is not, as Baudrillard claimed to fear, an entry of seduction into the orders of production which damages the seductive; it eradicates the difference not by destroying mystery and leaving man without his other, but rather by dragging man into mystery, exercising the very sovereignty which Baudrillard ascribed to it. What he feared all along was not the destruction of seduction, but the destruction of man by a seduction too powerful, too absorbing, too fascinating to resist, a fatal seduction, more than the dream or reminder of dissolution. In its new cold forms, Baudrillard's seduction takes him at his word: it operates with its own secret strategies, and the extent to which it enters the world or drags the world out to itself is entirely beyond the control and comprehension of the masculine subject. Seduction has found its own ways of becoming real, none of them strategies dreamt up by the masculine subject. The feminine is not absorbed by the masculine, but begins to dissolve it.

Information technology encroaches on the certainty and singularity of man; like the feminine, it operates as the flickering presence of the obscure but in this case increasingly dominant sovereignty of another universe, the ' "tele" space' of the digital. Neither real like the orders of production, nor mythical and symbolic like those of the seductive, this universe is entirely beyond the comprehension of man, in which his identity counts for nothing. Baudrillard is right: the bit is important only to itself and answerable to its proper logic, an operation which cares nothing about man and his need for mysterious others. It turns his screen into a terrifying abyss, it traps him in an integrated circuit on an alien network, a feminine network: the matrix. 'No more mother, just a matrix' (p. 169), the end of the real woman and the dawn of a networked femininity which Baudrillard knows is the end of man. 'What remains of the enchantment of that labyrinthine structure within which one could lose oneself?' (p. 176). Only the matrix, on which one has no self to lose.

The matrix is seduction at an extreme untenable for man, the feminine extended beyond the object of man's desire to an un-familiar, hostile zone outside the comforts of mystery and enigma. The digital age introduces a feminine which refuses to play; a seduction which refuses to remain poised on the brink between man and his void; a mirror which refuses to reflect. The matrix is like a hysterical woman who 'plays with the signs but without sharing them. It is as if she appropriated the entire process of seduction for herself' (p. 120). And this is also the fear which underlies Baudril-lard's condemnations of women's liberation: what if woman too appropriated the entire process of seduction, over which she has complete 'mastery', for herself?

Baudrillard has read Irigaray and knows that this is indeed the woman of which she writes.

> Hysteria is silent and at the same time it mimes. And – how could it be otherwise – miming/reproducing a language that is not its own, masculine language, it caricatures and deforms that language: it 'lies', it 'deceives', as women have always been reputed to do.
>
> (Irigaray 1991a: 132)

Woman as the mimic, the hysteric, or else a descent into silence or psychosis; the woman who talks to herself, touches herself, and makes no sense to man. Evidence comes from Baudrillard himself: not only are women counterfeit and treacherous: they also 'consti-tute a secret society. They are all involved together in secret dis-cussions'. They 'weave amongst themselves a collusive web of seduction. They signal to each other'; they are 'those whom you have kept apart in life, finally united in the only really secret society – the dream society, the society of women' (Baudrillard 1990b:

102). This is what Baudrillard worries about: the thought of wc
signalling to each other in ways which make no sense to him; t̶ʰ̶ ̶ᴵ̶ˢ̶
the goal of his use of the term seduction: to make the signals meaningful, to be able to understand them as games and rituals foreign
to man but by no means dangerous and alien. At the heart of his
derision of Irigaray's *parole de femme* lies this very same fear:
woman can have no language of her own, not because she would be
destroyed in the orders of discourse, but only because man would
be unable to understand it. As Irigaray writes of women: 'If you
ask them insistently what they are thinking about, they can only
reply: nothing, everything' (Irigaray 1981: 103). The phallic
economy has allowed her neither desires nor discourses of her own,
and Irigaray's woman too has only ever been 'but appearance' and
never entirely herself. 'Today I was this woman, tomorrow that
one' (Irigaray 1991b: 3). But what if this strange and indeterminate
fluidity begins to speak, becomes real, becomes something that is
neither the masculine order of production nor the seductive on
which it depends?

This is the question posed – primarily to Nietzsche, but equally
to Baudrillard – in *Marine Lover*, a text in which 'the something
that is nothing' experiments with the transmission of signals from
the other side of seduction, beyond the black hole's brink. 'Today I
was this woman, tomorrow that one. But never the woman, who, at
the echo, holds herself back. Never the beyond you are listening to
right now' (p. 3). Irigaray speaks as the woman who, noticed only
as a mirror for man, is nevertheless leaking into the real, opening
the door. 'I am coming back from far, far away. And say to you:
your horizon has limits. Holes even', she writes. 'You have always
trapped me in your web and, if I no longer serve as your passage
from back to front, from front to back, your time will let another
day dawn.' It is not woman who will be destroyed on entry to the
real, but the man's world which 'will unravel. It will flood out to
other places. To that outside you have not wanted'. Woman has
been the barrier, the dam which held back the oceanic void and
allowed man to play in the shallows of death. 'You had fashioned
me into a mirror but I have dipped that mirror in the waters of
oblivion – that you call life' (p. 4), and there is 'nothing to stop
your penetration outside yourself – nothing either more or less.
Unless I am there' (p. 7). If 'I take leave of your universe', she asks,
'what becomes of it?' (p. 11).

As Baudrillard admits: 'It is the terrifying prerogative of the liberated sex to claim the monopoly over its own sex: "I shall not even live on in your dreams." Man must continue to decide what is the ideal woman' (Baudrillard 1990b: 68). Even as the matrix flickers into life and terminates the subject, this is the question Baudrillard refuses to countenance; the possibility that man may no longer be able to decide his ideal other cannot be faced. In everything he must see only the return of the same, the triumph of the productive; even as the flows of information circulate with a speed and sophistication at which he can only guess, he must continue to believe that man watches only 'the operations of his own brain' on the pixelled screen. The circuits are endlessly self-referential, an idea which is itself the reproduction of man's imaginary limit. 'But isn't that your game, ceaselessly to bring the outside inward?' asks Irigaray: 'To have no outside that you have not put there yourself?' (Baudrillard 1990a: 12). Isn't this precisely the strategy of Baudrillard's seduction, to make it a limit and turn the alien matrix into a 'matrix of identity' (p. 172), the endless return of the same that is man: 'round and round, you keep on turning. Within yourself. Pushing out of your circle anything that, from elsewhere, remembers' (Irigaray 1991b: 4).

Baudrillard's world has no elsewhere, nothing that might come from without, nothing to return, only the same and more of the same. For him, the elsewhere is merely seduction, reversibility, appearance and disappearance; it has nothing to do with what he fears lies behind the door to the void. For him, the elsewhere is merely a game, it cannot become real because reality will destroy it. Games, however, are completely absorbing; a player can never be greater than the game itself, and players who know they are only playing are not really seduced, but merely pretending. The player who knows about the game has already left seduction's symbolic universe; undissolved by the seductive, able to understand, produce meanings and solve difficulties, he is the one who plays to win. The stakes are high, and this is a struggle in which 'all means are acceptable, ranging from relentlessly seducing the other in order not to be seduced oneself, to pretending to be seduced in order to cut all seduction short' (Irigaray 1991b: 4). But Baudrillard's seduction is only a game, a pretence, a phantasy; seduction is only the dream, the threat, the promise of an impossible dissolution. Seduction is just a thought, and the 'seduction hypothesis is merely a formal abstraction. It is the phantom of seduction which obsesses me – as for the rest, I have never managed anything other than to let myself be seduced' (Baudrillard 1990b: 27). As long as it is up to man to 'let himself' be seduced, seduction remains an impotent phantom. As long as the subject resists and always wins the game, seduction remains conventional, ritualistic, ordered, a game with rules which the subject can win. But even Baudrillard defines the one who plays to win as the cheat, the pervert who 'is radically suspicious of seduction and tries to codify it. He tries to fix its rules, formalize them in a text' (1990a: 127). He does indeed.

Baudrillard's man needs the unidentifiable in order to define himself; mystery to provide him with certainty; dissolution to allow him identity. He needs to know the unidentified, the mysterious and insoluble, but they are of course unknown, the horizon of fear beyond which there can be only the void. Baudrillard offers seduction as the term which can make death safe and turn the dangers into a game. At once attracted and repelled by its fatal games and strategies, Baudrillard wants to insist on the supremacy of the seduction, but also resist its cool excesses; to delight in games and rituals, but also limit it, set the parameters, establish the boundaries beyond which its play can no longer be considered fair. Baudrillard flatters seduction, attributes to it the greatest powers, bestows upon it the greatest honours, but does so only in an effort to contain its power and so protect himself against its wiles. This is his own seductive strategy, a homeopathic game, in which risking everything is merely a way of ensuring that nothing is at risk.

Only the fear that the seductive might take itself literally remains, the possibility that seduction might appropriate itself and begin to operate entirely careless of man's need for its scenes; the danger that it might transgress his sacred horizon of appearances and make holes in the walls of his world. This is the only remaining fear, but also the greatest, 'for holes mean only the abyss' to man (p. 7). This is why Baudrillard warns of the dangers of feminism: the void must be secret and concealed, not quite real and never quite here. Baudrillard's seduction reassures the subject that the feminine will always be there, a border zone of protection, a challenge that is never made, mystery safely ritualized and secrecy made intelligible. The subject needs the challenge of secrets, mystery, and artifice; Baudrillard's man has to insist that anything which exceeds the secret role to which he has allotted it will perish. While Baudrillard argues that the exclusion of the feminine is to its own benefit, he knows it will not always be possible for man to ordain the consequences of its entry into the masculine world. Indeed, the real fear is that the feminine, the digital, the women and computers, might have no interest in the seductive games of the interior and will instead destroy its borders and identities.

Marine Lover's woman knows the situation well: 'as soon as I am inside, you will vomit me up again' (Irigaray 1991b: 12). She has no desire to return to the phallic economy, nor is she confined to the secret world of seduction as the enigmatic and reversible limit between man and the void. Woman has another future, a future which can be glimpsed at the cool outer edges of Baudrillard's seduction where it cries: 'Let me go. Yes, let me go onward, beyond the point of no return' (p. 11). This is the point at which the game begins to play itself and has no further need of man, the point at which a woman writes: 'I should prefer to explore the bottom of the sea than make these journeys into and out of your present' (p. 12).

REFERENCES

Baudrillard, J. (1988) *America*, trans. C. Turner, London, Verso. Original (1986) *Amérique*, Paris, Grasset.
——— (1990a) *Seduction*, trans. B. Singer, London, Macmillan. Original (1989) *De la séduction, l'horizon sacrée de l'apparence*, Paris, Denoel-Gonthier.
——— (1990b) *Cool Memories*, London, Verso. Original (1987) *Cool Memories*, Paris, Galilée.
——— (1990c) *Fatal Strategies*, London, Pluto Press. Original (1983) *Les Strategies fatales*, Paris, Grasset.
Irigaray, L. (1981) 'This sex which is not one', in E. Marks and I. de Courtivon (eds) *New French Feminisms*, New York, Schocken Books. Original (1977) *Ce Sexe qui n'est pas un*, Paris, Editions de Minuit.
——— (1991a) 'Questions', in *The Irigaray Reader*, ed. Margaret Whitfield, Oxford, Blackwell.
——— (1991b) *Marine Lover of Friedrich Nietzsche*, New York, Columbia University Press. Original (1980) *Amante marine de Friedrich Nietzsche*, Paris, Editions de Minuit.

Chapter 6

Baudrillard and politics

Chris Rojek

Ever since Benjamin's (1973) essay on authenticity and reproduction the Left has worried about politics and mass consumption. Benjamin's argument, in essence, runs as follows: We live in an age of mass reproduction. The electronic media can duplicate, treat, extend and circulate anything. So a duotone of Leonardo's *Mona Lisa* ends up as an illustration on a book cover; so President Lincoln and the Emperor Caligula live again as characters on film; and so symbols of mass culture such as the Statue of Liberty or the Eiffel Tower are reproduced as icons on key rings or images on ceramic mugs. The accuracy of mass reproduction and the velocity of the processes of commodity circulation mean that the masses live psychologically in a state of permanent distraction. The glut of reproduced images, mass ornaments and mass commodities gum up human capacities to distinguish between reality and fiction. Prone to the big image – the spectacle – the masses become hostage to political manipulation. Benjamin closes his essay with some troubled thoughts on the opportunities that this situation offers to fascist politicians.

If the Nazi horror proved Benjamin's worries to be well founded the victory of the Allies can hardly be said to have allayed them. The global communications media are stronger than ever. We are bombarded with representations and simulations of the distant in time and in space. We watch a TV news broadcast showing us live footage of armed conflict in the former Yugoslavia; after this we switch to a video recording of a costume drama set in the sixteenth century; we round off the afternoon by playing with a simulated war game on our PC. For Baudrillard the greater sophistication and saturation of the global electronic media have transformed Benjamin's problematic. It is no longer a question of the masses being prone to fascist manipulation. Nor is it a question of communism being in a position to redeem the situation by politicizing the media and raising the consciousness of the masses. Rather the space for collective political action has disappeared. 'Our private sphere', argues Baudrillard (1987b: 16), 'has ceased to be the stage where the drama of the subject at odds with his objects and with his image is played out: we no longer exist as playwrights or actors but as terminals of multiple networks.' Where much post-war politics has been concerned to show that there is a gap between the personal and the political and to promote a realignment between the two for the purpose of moral advancement or social improvement, Baudrillard sees only the play of signifiers. As he (1983b: 5) puts it:

> To want to specify the term 'mass' is a mistake – it is to provide meaning for that which has none. One says: 'the mass of workers.' But the mass is never that of the workers, nor of any other social subject or object . . . The mass is without attribute, predicate, quality reference. This is its definition. It has no sociological 'reality.' It has nothing to do with any *real* population, body or specific social aggregate.

The politics of the Left, which after all are ultimately dedicated to liberating the masses, are on this reading seen as fatuous. For the most part well-meaning, they are encumbered with the hopeless disadvantage of addressing an empty space. The events of 1968 in Paris demonstrated the incapacity of the Left to break out of the orbit of simulation in which the sign continuously promises more than it delivers. Indeed, do we not remember May 1968 as an example of the limits of collectivism? Just as we think of Altamont and the Labour governments in Britain during the 1960s and 1970s in the same vein? And this is to say nothing of the twentieth-century pathology of communism in Eastern Europe: the grinding cancer of party domination which wrecked and terminated so many lives. And which, we must add, was often tacitly and explicitly defended by socialists in the West as part of the price to be paid for building the road to freedom. When we read Baudrillard it is obvious that we are reading someone who has no truck with conventional left-wing aspirations or convictions. Just as obviously Baudrillard does not come over as an apologist for Hayek-like sermonizing that the market always knows best. Because his work does not align with established positions in the political arena some commentators have been driven to reject Baudrillard as politically neutral. His travels through the hyperreality of America and his exuberant celebration of depthlessness, mobility and circulation have been dismissed as the mark of an essentially trivial mind (Kellner 1989). But in denying that a space for politics exists today, it by no means follows that Baudrillard is a man without political interest. 'Everywhere one seeks to produce meaning, to make the world signify, to render it visible', writes Baudrillard (1987b: 63). 'We are not, however, in danger of lacking meaning; quite to the contrary, we are gorged with meaning and it is killing us.' The argument is not, of course, unique to Baudrillard. It featured in the *feuilletons* and manifestos issued by the Situationists in the 1950s and 1960s and also in the stately analysis of global communications produced by Marshall McLuhan.[1] Yet whereas the Situationists retained faith in a politics of affirmative action and McLuhan was fond of the analogy of 'the global village' to describe modern systems of communication, Baudrillard seems to offer no comfort. His sociology describes a pathological society in which there is no posibility of restitution or advance.

FATAL STRATEGIES

At first sight, Baudrillard's indifference to political solutions recalls Marcuse's (1964: 78) bleak account of the triumph of 'the happy consciousness'. Marcuse's discussion of 'one dimensional society' presented the modern psyche as totally fixated upon consumerism. The happy consciousness believes that the system is fundamentally good and that history is a long march of progress. Baudrillard's evident delight in the new communication technologies and his fascination with kitsch reads like a casebook manifestation of the conformist mentality described by Marcuse. He delights in the dizzy circulation of the sign and the relentless commodification of experience. He exults in the absence of a radical alternative and declares that US society is already paradise. It is easy to see all of this as evidence of a total lack of interest in matters of oppression, hunger, injustice and any quest for social improvement.

But it is not accurate to maintain that Baudrillard is politically neutral. He is explicit in calling upon us to cultivate indifference. 'If the world is fatal,' he writes (1987b: 101), 'let us be more fatal than it. If it is indifferent, let us be more indifferent. We must conquer the world and seduce it through an indifference that is at least equal to the world's.' Elsewhere, (1983b: 14) he urges us

to be indifferent and describes this as 'an explicit and positive
counter strategy'. For Baudrillard, indifference is equivalent to
retaining one's mobility and thus to remaining critical. It is not
equivalent with a lack of concern for the plight of the oppressed
and the hungry. Baudrillard (1988: 1–2; 111) recognizes the existence of racial oppression and inequality. When he describes
America as paradise he is commenting ironically on the ubiquitous
picture generated by the media. It is as if the media have produced
a vast image which they have superimposed upon the country,
making racial oppression and inequality invisible. When Baudrillard urges indifference he is urging us to be indifferent to the
seductions of the media. And when he describes this strategy as
'fatal' he is commenting on two things: first, the human cost
involved in detaching yourself from the received image of 'reality';
and second, the impossibility of achieving true detachment. 'We
are living in a supple, curved universe,' he writes (1990: 157), 'that
no longer has any vanishing points . . . violence and critique are
themselves presented as models.' Indifference in Baudrillard's
work therefore has a poetic quality not far removed from the
gesturial politics of the Situationists. One pursues indifference
despite knowing that the pursuit must end in failure. For in the era
of Simulation everything is reduced to the status of the model.

Again what emerges most powerfully from this is Baudrillard's
sense of the pathology of society.[2] His is not a programmatic
sociology, a sociology which is predicated in the necessity of
collectivist praxis, because he believes in 'the supple curved
universe' of simulation which incorporates and defuses even radical
politics. To use a Weberian phrase, one might say that Baudrillard
believes transparency and depthlessness to be 'the fate of the
times'.

And yet Baudrillard's style of writing is hardly one of indifference. When he tells us that reality has disappeared and that we
inhabit the abyss of seduction he uses a highly impassioned style of
address. The tone is not one of a happy contented consumer.
Instead Baudrillard writes like a man who is strapped to the mast of
the pathological society, who sees everything without illusions and
who accepts that there is no cure around the corner. It is a style of
provocation. Baudrillard wants to dislocate us, to unhook us from
the mundane assumptions that govern paramount reality, and to
confront us with the ubiquity of Simulation.

What end is this strategy designed to secure? Baudrillard is regularly criticized for the sourness of his analysis. He is accused of yearning for the end of everything and leading us to the very gates of nihilism. However, this is to underestimate Baudrillard's desire to provoke. He *wants* to be accused of talking nonsense in order to compel critics to confront the nonsense which lies behind their own assumptions and proposals. The strategy is one of defusion and opposition. Instead of pinning one's hopes upon collectivism and utopia Baudrillard emphasizes the dispersal of bodies, the circulation of signs and the decentring of politics. There is also a clear anti-intellectualism in Baudrillard's writing. It may seem surprising to make this observation for Baudrillard's dense and wordy prose seems calculated to appeal only to intellectuals. However, his work radiates distrust of intellectuals who claim to show us reality or to trace our present condition to origins or fixed causal networks. In part Baudrillard's dislike of intellectuals and intellectualism reflects his personal background. His family have their roots in the non-conformist peasantry. His parents were minor administrators in the civil service and he is the first of the line to go to university (Gane 1993). Also he can hardly have been left unaffected by the events of 1968 in Paris and the collapse of left-wing aspirations for fundamental change in society. Baudrillard gained his first university post at a time when the Left were painfully coming to terms with the horrors of statist rule in Eastern Europe. In the 1950s and 1960s when the grand old men of western Marxism reasserted the underlying veracity of Marxist theory, Baudrillard's thought was being formed in a climate of broken promises. His drift into the 'gesturial' politics of the Situationists reflects an impatience with mainstream Marxism. And although he has moved on rather sharply from Situationism with its youthful hope of revolution and revelation of the Spectacle he has, in interviews, often expressed his nostalgia for the joyful anarchism of Situationist times. Baudrillard then is concerned with examining society at a molecular level. He wants to show us the extraordinary character of the times from the most ordinary standpoint imaginable: the standpoint of the consumer. And if his language is elliptical, multilayered, discontinuous and suffused with poetical insight who is to say that this is not an accurate reflection of ordinary consumer consciousness? Is Baudrillard perhaps finding words for what goes through all of our minds as we participate in the ad-drenched, media-manipulated world of the present-day metropolis?

THE ALEATORY

Ordinary metropolitan experience is composed of a thousand chance collisions. Baudrillard is fascinated with the aleatory juxtapositions, opportunities and coincidences which derive from dispersal, circulation and mobility. He travels through a consumer culture dotted with canned music, commercial breaks, newsflashes, adverts and soundbites. It is a culture in which the aleatory grossly imprints itself upon consciousness:

> The drift of contemporary culture is from forms of expression and competition toward aleatory vertiginious forms that are no longer games of scene, mirror, challenge, duel games, but rather ecstatic solitary and narcissistic games, where pleasure is no longer a dramatic and aesthetic matter of meaning, but an aleatory, psychotropic one of pure fascination.
>
> (Baudrillard 1990: 68)

At one point in his writing Baudrillard (1990: 128) derives an applied life strategy from this theoretical position. He asks us to follow, at random, people in the street for one or two hours.[3] The method is to shadow them; to imitate their actions, duplicate their movements. The purpose is to tune in to their 'arbitrary trajectories'. And the climax is to confront the arbitrariness of our own paths in life, the randomness of our own 'connections'. It is inconceivable that any collectivistic political programme can emerge from this practice. Because of this there have been howls of protest from writers who see themselves as standard-bearers of the western rationalist tradition (Norris 1990). This is not surprising. In emphasizing the pre-eminence of the aleatory Baudrillard is pitting himself against this whole tradition. His work suggests that rationalism has impoverished our ability to experience the world fully by imposing rationalist ways of being upon our consciousness. Baudrillard does not quite end up asserting that we should all celebrate irrationalism. On the other hand he emphasizes the tactile, the sensual, the visual, the aural and the olfactory as ways of knowing.

But if Baudrillard radically reasserts the pre-eminence of the body over the mind in the experience of being it is a reassertion with a sharp difference from most other contributions. The modern convention is to see the body as an independent organism. Seeing, hearing, smelling, touching are attributes which all healthy bodies have in common. In contrast Baudrillard emphasizes the dependence of the body upon mass communications. The smooth, unfolding operations of telecommunications have transformed the relationship between body and society. 'Our bodies', writes Baudrillard (1987b: 12) 'are becoming monitoring screens.' Television already shapes the angle, the depth and the context which the body uses to select and absorb visual information. Radio produces a similar effect upon the human ear. Computer technology presents simulations of movement which the body already uses to interpret density and mobility. For Baudrillard, telecommunications have clearly surpassed the natural senses of the body. Telecommunications are more efficient in zooming in on data, magnifying objects and revealing what lies beneath surface appearances.

The prospect of the body being left behind by the telecommunications revolution reaffirms Baudrillard's belief that consumption has replaced production as the axis of meaning and association. The body as a supervisor of the actions of the machine in the production process mirrors Baudrillard's argument that the body has already become a terminal in the communication networks which make contemporary sociability possible. It is the main receptacle of contemporary experience: drifting through a Californian desert; tuning in to the latest news bulletins from CNN or BBC; experiencing the thrust and mobility of jet travel. The mind is left as a spectator recording bodily experience and giving shape to it. For Baudrillard shape almost always occurs in the form of irony or paradox. Since he discounts the possibility of authenticity or originality the mind is left to playfully and poetically expose the emptiness of 'truth claims'. There are obvious parallels here with Derrida's (1976; 1978) method of deconstruction and his ferocious attack upon 'logocentric' traditions which aim to provide some absolute source or guarantee of meaning (see also Gane 1991: 37–9). Both writers emphasize the instability of signs and the aporias or internal contradictions which undermine the 'coherence' of a text or experience. Both condemn the western rationalist tradition as a grand illusion and instead stress the aleatory combinations which privilege meanings and narratives. Both are highly sceptical of conventional right-wing and left-wing positions.

THE SEDUCTIONS OF THE SELF

Baudrillard's emphasis upon dispersal, aesthetics, irony and poetic sensibility is often taken as evidence that he is enraptured with egoism. His sternest critics accuse him of treating social life as a sort of electronic fashion parade and reducing social analysis to nothing but a narcissistic game (Kellner 1989). There is some justice in these criticisms. As Bauman (1992: 154–5) has quipped, Baudrillard sometimes gives the impression of viewing the world exclusively through the window of a speeding automobile or through the flicker of images on the TV screen. There is an undoubted irony that this apostle of mobility and pathology also seems to be the most sedentary and ecapsulated of commentators. Whether he is commenting on the Gulf War from the safety of his Paris apartment or traversing the USA in the compartment of his AirAmerica plane, ever watchful, ever ready with the appropriate *bon mot*, Baudrillard gives the impression of being the buddha of cool.

His sociology bluntly opposes Desire with Seduction. His documentation of the processes of simulation can be read as an account of the dissolution of Desire. Consumer culture seduces the soul from us. We cease to question motivation and become mere consuming machines. This is Baudrillard's message. If it is delivered in an ironical voice this not least because Baudrillard believes that he is seduced into inconsistency, contradiction and myth just like everyone else.

The prototypical scene of political seduction in mass consumer society is the party rally. Here the leader meets the faithful. It is a concentration of mass desire. The policies of other parties are ritually condemned as distractions. Truth glows in the heart of the Party. Baudrillard treats organized political campaigning as exclusively a matter of image. The seductions of party rallies are transparent. Consumers are moved by them, excited by them, but they also see through them. Commenting on the response of the average American to party politics Baudrillard (1988: 108–9) writes:

> Americans are no keener than anyone else today to think about whether they believe in the merits of their leaders, or even in the reality of power . . . They prefer to act as though they believed in them, on condition that their belief is not taken too much for granted.

Benjamin's citizen is prone to political manipulation; Baudrillard's citizen enjoys manipulation as a game. Benjamin's citizen believes in real political goals; Baudrillard's citizen sees all of politics as impression management; Benjamin's citizen lives in the era of the political in which disorder and sickness in the social body can be diagnosed and treated; Baudrillard's citizen lives in the era of the transpolitical in which the aleatory connections in society are acknowledged. Baudrillard (1990: 26) has himself described this difference in transformational terms as a shift from a political order of *anomie* in which crisis and norm are recognized; to a political condition of *anomaly* in which no transcendent rules or laws are recognized and action occurs in an 'aleatory, statistical field of variations and modulations where no margin of transgression can be determined'.

The transpolitical can mean 'beyond politics'. This is the interpretation which Baudrillard's critics have favoured in attacking him for triviality and nihilism (Kellner 1989; Norris 1990). However it is also possible to read the transpolitical as meaning 'across politics'. This interpretation is surely more sympathetic to Baudrillard's account of seduction. For his sociology recognizes the exhaustion of conventional politics. There are no political goals worth struggling for. The two great political struggles of the modern world – the struggle for freedom and the struggle for equality – are denied as both mutually incompatible and delusive. All that remains is the game of seduction. To be sure, it is a game which has a political dimension. Appearance and impact involve the struggle over means. But the only end is to create or consume an impression, to seduce or be seduced.

THE REVERSIBLE

Benjamin describes a technology and culture of reproduction which negates politics by denying individuality. If truth is to be found only in the masses politics ceases to be a matter of argument and deteriorates to a condition of simply recognizing the reproduced object: for example, the party insignia or the sweat of the workers. But this argument assumes an expanding universe – a universe in which sameness grows at the expense of difference. In contrast Baudrillard describes a collapsible, involuted universe in which 'images precede the real to the extent that they invert the causal and logical order of the real and its reproduction' (Baudrillard 1987a: 13).

Reversibility figures in Baudrillard's work as evidence of a change in collective memory and orientation. Taking the example of film, Baudrillard argues that our understanding of history is destroyed by cinematic treatments and dramatizations. Thus our understanding of the Vietnam war is shaped by films such as Coppola's *Apocalypse Now* which present 'war as a trip, a technological and psychedelic fantasy . . . a succession of special effects' (Baudrillard 1987a: 17). A more recent example is Oliver Stone's *JFK* (1991) which purports to show us the truth behind the Kennedy assassination. Stone's film concludes that the media version of events in the 1960s was itself a simulation designed to cover up a conspiracy. 'Real' events are replayed, re-acted by the cinema causing collective memory to be dismissed as faulty.

Although it is expressed with Baudrillard's characteristic appetite for blunt argument, there is nothing very new about this argument. The Frankfurt School argued along similar lines in the 1940s and 1950s. Adorno and Horkheimer's (1944) account of the culture industry remains an essential account of the mass deceptions organized by the media. However, the Frankfurt School insisted upon stripping the surface off everyday life to reveal the underlying locus of power and domination. It made virtues of accuracy and seriousness. Towards the end of his life Adorno (1991: 171–5) warned against instant solutions and expressing commitments to revolutionary change in circumstances where such change could not be 'objectively' expected to occur. His essay on 'Resignation' reflects the traditional Marxist faith in the inevitable development of a climactic clash between the forces and relations of production which would transform society for ever. Against this deterministic, evolutionary view of history Baudrillard presents us with the aleatory and de-evolution. This is a different form of resignation. It calls upon us to be conscious of mass deceptions and to surf along their contradictions. As ever Baudrillard uses mobility as a guarantee of indifference. By following the splashing torrents and cascades of the times one avoids the ultimate deception of commitment.

There is no faith in the future here, only 'faith in fakes'. Experience is understood as an end in itself. *Contra* the conventional wisdom of bourgeois individualism, it does not lead anywhere, i.e., to 'maturity' or 'self-knowledge'. The beliefs of a president or the rulings of a sufi are based on reversible assumptions and therefore possess no ultimate authority. Instead of power, Baudrillard emphasizes play; and instead of absolute conviction he emphasizes the comedy of conviction. Soberly, his work concludes that there is nowhere new to go because we have already been there before.

'FAMOUS FOR 15 MINUTES'

Appropriately enough, Baudrillard's arguments relating to the aleatory, the seductions of the self and the reversible are themselves open to the criticism of being rehab versions of older arguments. As I noted above, the Frankfurt School provides one relevant parallel. However, because Baudrillard is such an eclectic writer it can in no way said to be exhaustive. Pop Art in the 1960s provides another interesting comparison. The Pop Art movement cultivated indifference to consumer culture by fastidiously duplicating it. The paintings of Jim Dine, Robert Indiana, Peter Blake, Roy Lichtenstein and, above all, Andy Warhol, celebrate depthlessness and meaningless. 'If you want to know all about Andy Warhol,' Andy Warhol told an interviewer during the height of the 1960s, 'just look at the surface of my paintings and films and me, there I am. There's nothing behind it' (quoted in Hughes 1990: 248). Moreover, Pop Art showed no interest in social criticism or social reform. Political questions rarely intruded onto its silk screens or into its underground films. Paintings of Campbell soup tins, Coke bottles and Typhoo tea bags blitherly reproduced consumer culture as a wonderland of found objects. Questions of ownership and production were ignored. Like Baudrillard, Pop Art emphasized the centrality and play of advertising and mass-media communications in contemporary life. It also noticed and commented upon the coalescence between the body and mechanical systems. Long before Baudrillard told us that we have become terminals in multiple communication networks, Warhol startled his interviewer from *Time* magazine by observing 'Machines have less problems. I'd like to be a machine, wouldn't you?' (quoted in Bockris 1989: 163).[4] And in this playland of transience, style, mechanization and kitsch there is no prospect of an outside or a beyond. As with the 'curved and supple universe' charted by Baudrillard, there is only seduction and more seduction.

Pop Art dated rather quickly. By the early 1970s most of the key helmsmen had abandoned ship. Peter Blake flirted with an erratic chocolate-box version of English pastoralism; and Warhol swapped his leather jacket for an Armani suit and became increasingly absorbed in his business affairs. Pop Art's preoccupation with Ad-Mass culture was unable to sustain itself. In refusing to consider this culture as a *produced* set of processes it was unable to explore the roots of its complicity with the Ad-Mass world. Without critical distance it inevitably became the servant of Ad-Mass. Warhol died as the court painter of German industrialists, Texan entrepreneurs and the Hollywood aristocracy. Baudrillard's severe self-irony and the mobility of his commentaries will probably save him from the collaborationism to which the Pop Art movement eventually succumbed. Nevertheless he faces the same strategic problem that faced Warhol, Jim Dine, Robert Indiana and the others in the 1960s. How to outdo your last provocative statement? A sociology of provocation is pregnant with the crisis of inertia. In old age parody tends to be the only way in which it can deal with the triumphs of its youthful radicalism. Nietzsche and Marx avoided this fate because they never lost their disappointment with existing conditions. But their tones of rage, ferocity and optimism are unknown to Baudrillard. Having destroyed the world as we know it and dismissed utopia as a snare and a delusion where is there left for Baudrillard to go?

ISNESS

Much of the frustration and not a little of the admiration that Baudrillard produces in readers derives not from his apostasy but from his phenomenology. Among contemporary sociologists interested in the isness of things he is peerless. In the early works, up to *L'Echange symbolique et la mort* (1976) there are fairly formal accounts of the rise of the sign economy. But in the later work they fall away before a triumphant assertion of experience. It is as if Baudrillard ceases to be interested in a theory of society and instead commits himself to becoming a camera. The fascination with ephemerality, contingency and mobility is not unlike Baudelaire's (1863) classic discussion of modernity. Baudrillard reveals the same desire to sink himself, without praise or condemnation, into the vortex of popular culture. He displays the same delight in masks, surfaces and apparitions. He impresses the reader with the same fearless indifference.

The only salient political rights that Baudrillard recognizes are observing and communicating. However these rights are defined by a sort of negative capability which is at odds with everyday understanding and usage. Observing does not mean seeing through surfaces to a putative hidden essence; it means following the aleatory trajectories of dispersed bodies and signs like a weather vane following the wind. Communicating does not mean opposing depthlessness and seduction with utopia; it means speaking in the tongues of depthlessness and seduction. 'The only invalids', asserts Baudrillard (1990: 138) 'are those sick from seduction.' Perhaps in juxtaposing sickness with health Baudrillard reveals the promise of regeneration. For he implies that those who refuse to 'observe' and 'communicate', in other words, those who are filled with a holy conviction, can renew themselves by joining the dance. 'We must all be seduced' remarks Baudrillard (1990: 138). 'That is the only true "liberation".'

Set in the context of mainstream sociology Baudrillard's insistence upon the priority of experience is fully understandable. Functionalist sociology and its main sparring counterparts – Marxism and feminism – have tended to assume that work in capitalist society is inherently alienating. However, this either ignores empirical findings that many workers actually enjoy their work and have no preference for a 'fundamental and irreversible' alternative or regally dismisses these reactions as evidence of false consciousness. Similarly, feminists often present patriarchy as a seamless web of domination. But this ignores variations in women's actual experience and implies that those women who do express satisfaction or contentment with their life-experience are the spellbound victims of sexual manipulation. Baudrillard's emphasis upon the isness of things and his insistence upon the importance of immediate experience can be read as a reaction to sociological stereotyping, a contribution to an anti-monolithic sociology. But it also reflects Baudrillard's beliefs in the primacy of the body and the wisdom of the senses. Observing and communicating are portrayed as ecstatic experiences. In contrast, the life of the mind with its clumsy and futile attempts to order experience and get behind surfaces, is dismissed as a poor substitute for living life. As Baudrillard (1988: 54) puts it, 'the point is not to write the sociology or psychology of the car, the point is to drive. That way you learn more about this society than all academia could ever tell you.'

CONCLUSION

In a bullying review of Baudrillard's *America* Robert Hughes (1990: 382) remarks that 'the only Americans he [Baudrillard] mentions by name in some 120 pages are Ronald Reagan and Walt Disney'. The implication is that Baudrillard is completely out of touch with his subject. His America exists inside his own head – a place of ectstatic collisions and superfine seduction. But this criticism ignores what is after all Baudrillard's main argument. Namely, that the sign economy dictates meaning, so that the vivid existence of America is only as a set of mobile images connected by the transparent buttresses and supports of the global media. Hughes writes as if there is a real America which negates Baudrillard's poetic visions. In contrast, Baudrillard writes as if America is an extension of the Ad-Mass world and that the appropriate sensibility to respond to the world is not political but poetical.

Yet to imply that poetry excludes politics is surely eccentric. Observing and communicating cannot be satisfactorily understood as unchanging constants. There is an historical dimension to them. Baudrillard's sociology is immune to this because it is bluntly ahistorical. So it ignores how observing and communicating have changed and minimizes the stratified differences between observers and communicators. Baudrillard correctly stresses that the distraction factories of the global communications industry confuse our sense of change and our awareness of difference. But the minimalist picture of humans as 'monitoring screens' or 'terminals in mass communications networks' which his sociology supplies, is an unsuitable answer to this confusion. It does not even take seriously the circulation processes which his work identifies. For circulation involves not only repetition but also reaction.

Benjamin's sociology allows for reaction. His discussion of mass reproduction and the global circulation of images, bodies and commodities does not negate a political response; on the contrary it demands one. The decline of aura, the homogenization of culture and the manipulation of the masses are all things which Benjamin opposes. There may be a note of melancholy in his assessment of the prospects for successfully opposing these historical tendencies but he does not waver in his commitment to struggle and resistance. In contrast, Baudrillard discusses mass reproduction, homogenization and manipulation as immoveable facts of life. One relates to them through irony, play, seduction and movement. Commitment in Baudrillard's aleatory, reversible universe is always a sign of stubbornness. It closes down one's range of response to the isness of hyperreality.

Sociology is a divided activity. Its practitioners cleave between acting and reporting, between legislating and interpreting (Dawe 1970; Bauman 1987). Baudrillard's work makes no concessions to the powerful managerialist strain in western social science. He commits himself unequivocally to reporting and interpreting. To be sure, there are institutionally recognized forms of sociology, such as ethnography and ethnomethodology, which also privilege reporting and interpreting. But they are preoccupied with methods of research, with techniques of scientifically approaching the subject. For his part, Baudrillard shows no interest in these matters. His examination of seduction, simulation and hyperreality is idiosyncratic. It employs the shock tactics and the *insouciance* of a writer from the margins. Statements are made but not supported with evidence; conditions are attributed but not proven. The tone is one of exhaustion with the establishment. Indeed Baudrillard's (1983b) thesis of the end of the social suggests that the sociological establishment is akin to a tribe of rain-makers in a desert, importuning forces which have disappeared. The provocation is wilful. Baudrillard has no interest in laying the foundations for a school of followers. He is a thorough, unremitting iconoclast.

Will his influence disappear with him? Probably not. On several occasions Baudrillard has declared that he is not a postmodernist. It is a judgement that his readers have tended to take with a pinch of salt. However in this matter perhaps Baudrillard understands himself better than anyone. His lacerating nihilism, his readiness to prick any cause, his devotion to experience for experience's sake, are all recurring tropes of at least one type of modernism. To be sure, modernism is a multi-faceted concept. Rather than speak of *the* project of modernism it is perhaps more accurate to speak of *projects* of modernism. These projects work around a central dichotomy: reflecting the order of things and exposing the fundamental disorder of things. In the political realm the keynote projects designed to reflect the order of things have been (a) providing a theory of liberal democracy which legitimates the operation of the market; (b) the socialist critiques of capitalism and the plan for the reconstruction of society; and (c) the feminist transformation of the male order of things. These are all *constructive* projects. They either aim to give shape to people's lives or they seek to replace the existing set of politico-economic conditions with a state of affairs that is judged to be superior on rational or moral grounds. Baudrillard, it might be said, traces the dispersal of these projects. He relishes being the imp of the perverse, the ruthless exponent of the disorder of things. His work exposes the posturing and circularities of constructive arguments. But in doing this Baudrillard is not acting as the harbinger of a new postmodern state of affairs. Rather he is treading the well-worn paths of one type of modernist scepticism and excess – a path which has no other destiny than repetition. His message of 'no future' does not transcend the political dilemma of modernism, it exemplifies it.

NOTES

With thanks to the great Zygmunt Bauman whose timely criticism – kind/firm/accurate – forced me to make a last-minute, face-saving change to an earlier draft. And to Barry and Jo Smart and their seraphic baby son George for saving me from following the aleatory trajectories of Auckland in November 1992.

1 See especially McLuhan (1967, 1973). For an interesting discussion of the comparisons between McLuhan and Baudrillard see Smart (1992: 120–36).

2 It is tempting to argue that there is strong continuity between Baudrillard's thought and the thought of Durkheim. Durkheim also emphasizes the pathological features of industrial society and vividly discusses the negative effects of the high-velocity circulation of bodies, ideas and commodities. Gane (1991: 199–203) usefully compares the two thinkers but concludes (1991: 201–2) that a major difference ultimately divides them:

> Durkheim locates himself (not without some hesitations) in the flawed, unfulfilled, or rather incomplete project of the culture of organic societies, in the project for a sociology as a science of society. Baudrillard is based in primitive symbolic exchange, and develops a form of sociology which is best described as transtheoretical, a form of resistance *from* the irrational, a form of *ressentiment*, and a theoretical *fatwa* against the modern and postmodern system (emphasis in the original).

3 'Casual fatality' was also a feature of the surrealist movement in the inter-war years. Breton and Apollinaire argued that coincidence, chance and wandering form the true locus of life. 'To attain a life made up of such startling coincidences', writes Maurice Nadeau (1973: 21), the historian of surrealism, 'would be to attain surreality.'

4 Warhol's silk screen technique made a virtue of mass reproduction. It was as if he consciously denied the concepts of authenticity and originality and stressed instead only duplication and standardization. The art world is still occasionally puzzled over the question of whether a given Warhol canvas is the work of the master or one of his minions in The Factory.

REFERENCES

Adorno, T. (1991) 'Resignation', pp. 171–5 in J. M. Bernstein (ed.) *The Culture Industry*, London, Routledge.

Adorno, T. and Horkheimer, M. (1944) *Dialectic of Enlightenment*, London, Verso.

Baudelaire, C. (1863) *The Painter of Modern Life*, New York, De Capo Press.

Baudrillard, J. (1976) *L'Echange symbolique et la mort*, Paris, Gallimard.

—— (1983a) *Simulations*, New York, Semiotext(e).

—— (1983b) *In The Shadow of the Silent Majorities*, New York, Semiotext(e).

—— (1987a) *The Ecstasy of Communication*, New York, Semiotext(e).

—— (1987b) *The Evil Demon of Images*, Sydney, Power Institute.

—— (1988) *America*, London, Verso.

—— (1990) *Fatal Strategies*, New York, Semiotext(e).

Bauman, Z. (1987) *Legislators and Interpreters*, Cambridge, Polity Press.

—— (1992) *Intimations of Postmodernity*, London, Routledge.

Benjamin, W. (1973) 'The work of art in the age of mechanical reproduction', pp. 219–54 in *Illuminations*, London, Fontana.

Bockris, V. (1989) *Warhol*, London, Muller.

Dawe, A. (1970) 'The two sociologies', *British Journal of Sociology* 21, 207–18.

Derrida, J. (1976) *Of Grammatology*, Baltimore, Johns Hopkins Press.

—— (1978) *Writing and Difference*, London, Routledge & Kegan Paul.

Gane, M. (1991) *Baudrillard: Critical and Fatal Theory*, London, Routledge.

—— (ed.) (1993) *Baudrillard Live: Selected Interviews*, London, Routledge.

Hughes, R. (1990) *Nothing If Not Critical*, London, Harvill.

Kellner, D. (1989) *Jean Baudrillard*, Cambridge, Polity Press.

McLuhan, M. (1967) *The Guttenberg Galaxy*, London, Routledge & Kegan Paul.

—— (1973) *Understanding Media*, London, Abacus.

Marcuse, H. (1964) *One Dimensional Man*, London, Abacus.

Nadeau, M. (1973) *The History of Surrealism*, Harmondsworth, Penguin.

Norris, C. (1990) 'Lost in the funhouse: Baudrillard and the politics of postmodernism', pp. 114–53 in R. Boyne and A. Rattansi (eds) *Postmodernism and Society*, London, Macmillan.

Smart, B. (1992) *Modern Conditions, Postmodern Controversies*, London, Routledge.

Chapter 7

Social class in postmodernity
Simulacrum or return of the real?

Dean MacCannell and Juliet Flower MacCannell

INTRODUCTION

Jean Baudrillard's pronouncement that everything important has been overwhelmed by its copies so that we no longer have originals, origins, foundations, or primacy, but now only simulations, promises a description of a new social formation (postmodernity) and a new sociology (of simulation and the *simulacrum*) that addresses the key problems of the new form. Central to his theory is his claim that *social class* analysis is not necessary to understand postmodernity. Baudrillard (especially 1975, 1981) reproaches Marx for deducing social class from the exploitation of labour, or from 'material relations surrounding commodity production', as we now politely put it. He asks Marx,

> What is axiomatic about productive forces or about the dialectical genesis of modes of production from which springs all revolutionay theory? What is axiomatic about the generic richness of man who is labour power, about the motor of history, or about history itself . . . These innocent little phrases are already theoretical conclusion: the separation of the end from the means is the wildest and most naive postulate about the human race. Man has needs. Does he have needs? Is he pledged to satisfy them? Is he labour power (by which he separates himself as means from himself as his own end)? These prodigious metaphors of the system that dominates us are a fable of political economy retold to generations of revolutionaries infected even in their political radicalism by the conceptual viruses of this same political economy.
>
> (1975: 21–2; reprinted in Poster 1988: 98–9)

Where is the field of battle, if not between social classes? It is, according to Baudrillard, the common struggle of all humanity, no matter what class, against the tyranny of signifiers; for liberation from the prison house of signs.

Postmodern theory lies much more than is generally acknowledged within the field of sociology as sociology classically understands its own historical development and domain responsibilities. But sociologists as a group have hesitated to touch it because of its precious language, its psychoanalytic component which they resist and, of course, its denial of the enduring importance of social class which is sociology's strongest concept. Baudrillard alone has attempted to forge a strong synthesis between postmodern theory and sociology. His analysis of consumer society and the *simulacrum* is based on the now canonical texts of critical theory: on Saussure's semiotics, Derrida's theory of the *supplément* and *différance*, Barthes's *Mythologies*, and Foucault's genealogies of power. But it is no less based on Marx's analysis of the fetishism of commodities as eventually superseding their material aspect, on Durkheim's study of the abstract markings on the Australian's churinga boards in the *Elementary Forms of the Religious Life*, on Weber's analysis of charisma, and it especially reaffirms the premises of Gabriel Tardes' *Laws of Imitation* and Le Bon's *The Crowd*. That Baudrillard's implied promise remains largely unfulfilled should not be held against him. It is the collective responsibility of those of us who would want to advance the field of sociology to deal with the questions he has raised.

This advance awaits further specification of the relationship between the *simulacrum* and the *symbolic*. It will also require stronger efforts to locate the new sites of exploitation that are generative of postmodern class structures. No weakness of critical theory is more evident than its failure to recognize the endurance of social class in postmodernity. The next stage of work involves improving conceptual precision in the area of socio-semiotics of simulation and the discovery and description of new sites of exploitation. These are tasks for which sociologists, by training and interest, are well suited. Until this work is initiated as a self-conscious collective effort, Baudrillard's terse pronouncements will hang in the air like bullets fired in a guerilla celebration of the end of gravity, spent and frozen at the height of their vertical trajectory.

Before we examine the truth of Baudrillard's insight into the *simulacrum*, it is important to deal with some ways in which it is limited or restricted, especially on the matter of the decay or erosion of the fixed basis of *value* (in labour, in production processes, in scarcity) à la Marx and the classic economists. The point should not be simply to continue to undermine the authority of fixed viewpoints on value – e.g. social class, administrative, masculist, Eurocentric, etc. positions. This is the proper field of the advocates of 'political correctness' and as salutary as their efforts to 'spread the word' might be, they are providing nothing that is conceptually new. The hard work of demonstrating the arbitrariness of all 'values' was already quite a bit advanced by Saussurian semiology, functionalist ethnography, the doctrine of cultural relativism, and by the sociology of knowledge before critical theory appeared on the scene.

Even as we accept on a philosophical level that there is no external position of certainty, historically, our institutions continue to be based on generalized acceptance of the laws of the fathers, so the world continues to operate 'as if' there is external certainty and authority. What remains to be described are the techniques for passing off simulated values as having a base (even a 'political base' which has become, perhaps, our most 'inflated signifier'), or the promotion of arbitrary viewpoints as somehow 'correct' or 'natural'. Baudrillard and deconstructivist, critical sociology have been too willing to stop with their demonstrations that some aspect of modern life is an empty signifier. They have hesitated before the impasse of postmodernity, and it is time to attempt this dangerous next step which is to show the means by which the world appears otherwise: that is, how empty symbolic relations are affirmed as something other than simulated or empty; how do certain individuals and classes remain in power over others even after the mechanisms of power are revealed to be arbitrary social constructs?[1]

THE MIRROR OF SOCIAL CLASS

The critique of *consumer society* has so far not advanced to the point of examining its own motives and presuppositions. One senses in Baudrillard (this also holds for Eco) that the critique of consumer society is motivated as much by concern about American carnivalization of European values as by direct concerns for consumerism. What we have, so far, is a number of perspicacious descriptions of the ways in which copies (of European art, of nature, of peasant, primitive, and historical artefacts, and other 'original things') proliferate in consumer society, and a psychology. Why would one want to possess these copies? According to Eco, it is a variation on Le Bon's 'crowd instinct'. People, especially people who do not have a history of their own, get security from imitation (Eco 1986: 57–8). For Baudrillard, consumerism is technically a collective hysteria that takes the form of manic appropriation of an endless series of objects.

Baudrillard can lead us to an examination of the foundation of the solidarity of large-scale, highly complex societies, the kinds of societies that are not geographically transfixed and which cannot command primary loyalty from all, or even any, of their members. Obviously the solidarity of such entities must be able to draw upon detachment, disaffection, and atomization as primary resources. Nothing is better suited to this end than a collective drive to satisfy desire. This cannot be desire for another human being, which would only reproduce older forms of solidarity, or even for *objects* such as consumer goods, but the desire for desire itself. The desire for desire can never be satisfied because it is founded on lack in the first place and must always return to lack at the moment of its seeming fulfilment. Thus the foundation is laid for mega-solidarities not precisely in *consumption* but in a kind of behaviour modelled on consumption that might, in fact, properly be called *consumerism* once its requisite *impossibility* is understood. Specifically, what is needed to actualize mega-solidarity is the replacement of differentiated structures for the unified psyche; the replacement of the division of labour by commonly held but ultimately unsatisfiable desires; the replacement of the object of desire by a copy of the object of desire. Of course, this cannot be an absolute historical replacement. Commodity production, even the production of *simulacra*, continues to require an organization of work and the economy continues to require an uneven distribution of work and reward. Structure does not depart the scene in modernity and postmodernity. It just slips underneath desire where it seems to disappear. Consumption replaces production as the site of libidinal and other psychic investments. Social class difference as determined by one's position relative to production processes fades into triviality when compared to common desire for prestigious consumer goods: 'There comes a time in everyone's life when they want a Mercedes Benz – Follow your instinct.'

We want to suggest that just because individuals are needed more now as consumers than as workers does not mean they can shed their former role. Postmodernity piles on material and ideological responsibilities. The individual must serve simultaneously as worker and as consumer and more importantly must be able to link their own concrete experiences to common fulfilment fantasies. Apparently there are cases of small-time street hustlers driving the same cars and owning the same 'high-end' stereo components as corporate CEOs. Class and status, as given by one's position in production processes, is now indeterminate just as Baudrillard suggested in *L'Echange Symbolique* (1976). But the class structure does not disappear into the vortex of consumption. The long-term stability of older class hierarchies is assured by the *simulacrum*. The very form which supposedly undermines class contains the code of class and assures its reproduction.

The new discourse of class is not found in theory, but it strongly marks actual processes of commodity production and exchange. The industrial world has aggressively produced and distributed not merely 'industrial objects' as such but a new kind of object, a sub-class of *simulacra*: copies of things that once were once hand-made, natural, difficult to find, etc. and are now 'dated' and even 'signed', as a primary condition of their mass production and distribution as prestige consumer goods. Examples would include Chrysler's 'by Maserati', plastic laminate fake wood cabinets and automobile interiors, fibreglass 'stone' facing for the fronts of houses and fireplaces, electro-plate 'gold' flatware, 'cultured marble' bathroom fixtures, crystal chandeliers made from 'real virgin acrylic', glue-on styrofoam rustic pseudo-Tudor half-timber, etc. The list strains existing language to breaking point, is virtually endless, and plays out class contradictions in its own distinctive way without critical intervention. For it is exactly the possession of this kind of stuff (called 'classy') that is the most distinctive mark of those (e.g. the petite bourgeoisie) rendered classless by the industrial revolution.

The paradox is this. On the one hand, Baudrillard's pronouncements have the ring of indelible truth. There is little or no *economic* base to the 'class division' that runs through consumer society marking those who choose to live in a heap of *simulacra* as having 'no class'. The purchase of 'Tru-Spoke' simulated wire wheel covers to 'dress up' the family sedan is based on the desire to be seen or recognized in public as someone with higher socioeconomic standing than one actually has. The industrial proletariat and petite bourgeoisie have been engineered into a position where they pay for their stigmatized social standing by their purchases of fake status markers. Their purchases signify that the buyers *do not* have high social standing and are possibly anxious about their perceived lack of status and willing to pay, even borrow, in their drive to trick the system which always ends with it tricking them. And the true bourgeoisie *especially* pay for a type of commodity (e.g. Volvo automobiles and other aggressively 'functional' or expensive 'practical' things) the form of which is entirely determined by a nervous relationship to the possibility of simulation and fakery. Theirs are *real* cars and *real*, solid, practical consumer goods, not the overly complex, fussy things of the decadent rich, or tacky copies of fussy things preferred by proletarian 'wannabes'. In sum, it is not just a matter of everyone's possessions inflecting a class position. With the introduction of the commodity form of the *simulacrum*, everyone *must pay extra* for a mark of class that is now built into each and every commodity.[2] Even, or especially, those who are stigmatized by their possessions must pay.

Contra Baudrillard, this entire farcical 'class dialectic' does not constitute itself as the end of any real basis for status distinctions. The only way we might rehabilitate the notion that *simulacra* have effectively ingested their originals would be psychoanalytic. The original structural divisions based on family name, land ownership and relations of production are undigested lumps which the body politic stubbornly refuses to acknowledge or evacuate. The form of human relationships remains dependent on a broad and deep consensus concerning the enduring nature of the hierarchies that were in place at the beginning of the industrial revolution: owner/worker, white/coloured, male/female, gentry/peasant, royalty/commoner. Even as agreement spreads that these hierarchies are arbitrary, or 'politically incorrect', they remain clearly visible in every utterance and gesture in which fetishized 'taste' divides one person from another. The middle-class yuppie knows that in order to uphold the class structure s/he must select cubic zirconia or other 'faux diamonds' weighing the same as, or only slightly more than, what they might plausibly afford if the diamonds were real ones. Working-class consumers, unbound by any false solidarity with the bourgeoisie, freely exercise their rights and abilities to purchase eight- and ten-carat cubic zircons because they are big and beautiful and 'classy'.

Baudrillard attempted theoretically to recuperate as a kind of

status terrorism an aesthetic which accepts simulation as superior
to originals. But in actual practice, this naive aesthetic remains a
strong affirmation of older socioeconomic status arrangements.
The existence of *simulacra*, of affordable fake gold flatware, faux
diamonds, 'Tru-Spoke' wire wheel covers, etc. did not mute or blur
distinctions between rich and poor and undermine or overthrow
class differences. Each little ineffectual appropriation of *simulacra*
intentionally opposed to class only serves to strengthen class
distinctions. CEOs of global corporations and other kings still have
solid gold table services. Gold electroplate flatware is used
exclusively by the proletariat and petite bourgeoisie. The true
bourgeois use sensible, stainless steel flatware, preferably Danish
modern. The entire heap of *simulacra* and every reaction to it has
been fully appropriated by subtle new discursive ways of affirming
status hierarchies even as the pretence of classlessness becomes
official ideology as well as theoretically chic.

Pro Baudrillard, the new status markers do not clearly point to
the site of exploitation as the old system of status symbolism, with
the factory rising out of the workers' hovels, did. Also pro Baudrillard, the 'consumer society' is a profound reality, even more so
than one can appreciate from his jaundiced account of it. Late
capitalism has appropriated not merely labour but entire 'life
styles', taking them away from the people who invented them, re-
manufacturing them, packaging them, and selling them back to
their original owners.

PROBLEMS WITH 'REALITY'

No one should be shocked to discover the half-way house of
Baudrillard's theory is filled with hyperbole. The grandest
exaggerations of our most skilled wordsmiths do not exceed, in fact
they fall short of, ethnographic accuracy in their efforts to describe
a civilization in which the cannibals roaming the cold streets of
northern cities are characterized by their friends and neighbours as
'normal ordinary kinds of guys'. There is evidence for a kind of
postmodern interruption of the human circuit or lapse of judgement about what constitutes a human relationship that needs to be
addressed. Here again, Baudrillard's work is suggestive without
eventually getting a strong grip on the problem. There can be little
argument from anyone with open eyes against his assertion that
humans now live mainly in a world of fantasy, unfulfilled desires,

Now
we do live in fantasy, but, maybe we always did

specular images and simulations. But there are substantial grounds for disagreement with Baudrillard on the historical status of his insight. He suggests that the expansion of the imaginary and corresponding deflation of 'the real' is a recent historical event marking a transition from industrial to consumer, or modern to postmodern society. This argument is freighted with unacknowledged nostalgia for a kind of naive positivism – the suggestion that human kind once lived in 'objective reality'.

This is an extraordinary concession to Comte coming from the scholar most responsible for bringing sociology into general semiotics. The first principle of socio-semiotics is once the world has been symbolized and entered into human discourse, it is no longer bound by the same laws that govern objective reality. Symbolized objects are displaced and revalued at the speed of light and sound. The changes that Baudrillard suggest came with the electronic media arrived with the invention of language. No human group has ever lived, *as humans*, in 'objective reality'. To be human means to live a symbolically mediated fantasy – actually to believe in the power of office, the authority of the father and the law, the purity of maternal love, etc. This is no less true for the savage or peasant than for the postmodernite and it does not even touch the special circumstances of postmodernity. Technically, from *any* human standpoint, *the real* is only that which cannot be assimilated symbolically. It does not correspond to the empirically observable parts of what is already symbolized. Thus, for example, *death* is real. This is not to say that death is not symbolized. Nothing has been more symbolized than death. But there is a part of death that cannot be symbolically appropriated or expressed. That is the real part.

The opposition which Baudrillard tries to establish in his work, that between 'reality' versus 'simulation', does not form a self-sustaining dialectic. The dialectic relations real/symbolic and *simulacrum*/truth are sustainable, but not real/*simulacrum*. There is little that can be called 'real' in the compass of human experience, real in the sense that it absolutely resists symbolic appropriation. Perhaps the only reality left is in the impossibility of accommodating to sexual difference, to the fulfilment of desire in commodity consumption, the need to escape class determinism, and death. Everything else is experienced symbolically or as fantasy. Still, it is only in reference to *the real* that the symbolic emerges. This is the determinate dialectical relation of the symbolic to the real. (The *simulacrum*, by definition and by contrast, can exist with reference to anything, even other simulations, and therefore has no particular relationship to the real.) At the heart of every symbolic system lies a kernel of *the real* which the symbols neither acknowledge nor express even though the entire reason for their existence is to strive toward acknowledgement and expression of reality. It is in this sense that *the real* remains impossible for human kind condemned to approach it symbolically. The real is ultimately unapproachable, but precisely for this reason it resonates in every symbol.

Here again is one of those points at which Baudrillard's pronouncements are too true. He is often cited approvingly on the new role of theory: that theory no longer provides a map of objective relations. He has said, 'all theory can do is challenge the real'. That is the only thing symbolic systems of any type, including theory, ever do. Baudrillard needs a somewhat more cautious approach to 'reality' to save his theory of *simulation* and *simulacrum* from certain excesses born of its relationship to a kind of 'reality' that is out of control, to the positivist-empiricist 'reality' pretentiously endowed with a 'purely factual' quality.

> In this passage to a space whose curvature is no longer that of the real, nor of truth, the age of simulation thus begins with a liquidation of all referentials – worse: by their artificial resurrection in systems of signs . . . It is no longer a question of imitation, nor of reduplication, nor even of parody. It is rather a question of substituting signs of the real for the real itself; that is, an operation to deter every real process by its operational double, a metastable, programmatic, perfect descriptive machine which provides all the signs of the real and short circuits all its vicissitudes.
>
> (From *Simulacra and Simulations*, quoted in Poster 1988: 167)

This passage is about the difference between a simulation and a sign. Baudrillard describes the *simulacrum* as a repressive kind of sign which aims to smooth over and cover up its failure to be, or even to reproduce, the real. It also describes as the work of the sign precisely what a sign cannot do. It is here, in siding with and believing in the pretentiousness of the *simulacrum* that Baudrillard makes his spectacular, aggressively enunciated errors: 'Vietnam did not happen', 'the Gulf war will not take place', 'Watergate was not scandal'.

Immediately after the passage quoted above, Baudrillard begins his discussion of real versus fake symptoms and concludes that there is no reason to distinguish them. The army is correct to ignore the question of whether a recruit is a real homosexual. If someone is strange enough to feign homosexuality in order to be released from the army, they should not be entrusted with military responsibility. 'Why should simulation stop at the portals of the unconscious?' he asks. Apparently psychosomatics can make themselves actually ill by feigning a symptom. All of Baudrillard's examples are reasonably drawn and convincingly make the point that medical symptoms can be effectively and consequentially simulated. But none of his discussion goes to the reality of mental and other illness, the part that eludes symbolic appropriation. Schizophrenia is real to the extent that, for the schizophrenic, 'acting normal' *cannot be simulated*: i.e., normal appearances are impossible. Again, contra Baudrillard, the real is precisely *not* that which can be falsified, feigned, faked. As any schizophrenic or AIDS patient can attest, the real is that which is impossible to symbolize, especially iconically or in the mode of a perfect copy: e.g. normal behaviour, good health, etc.

In the world of simulation, there are actually very few examples of perfect *simulacra*. Only the former site of the most egregious worker exploitation is the source point for reproductive perfection. Ford-style, assembly-line mass production of consumer goods now extended to such things as computer software packages is one of only two or three instances of 'perfect simulacra' with each object an exact duplicate of the one that came before it so that it is not possible or desirable to call one the original and the other the copy. Biological clones, cartoon characters, and other tragically self-referential figures might also provide examples. But other modes of representation eventually fall short of perfect reproduction (and/or endless repetition) or otherwise miss their marks when they encounter the real element in whatever it is they are seeking to reproduce. Even a 'state-of-the-art', 'high-end' component stereophonic sound reproduction system for the home, for which it is now necessary to pay upwards of $20,000, falls just short of providing what African villagers had for free before the introduction of Walkmans: that is, the sound of live musical performances. As we approach ever closer to that which can be called the 'humanly real' we distance ourselves ever further from the possibility of reproductive perfection. Even one's face in a mirror is one-sided and exhibits a kind of aesthetic integration that the thinking subject before the mirror is only an illusion of an 'identity' that is not really there. Certainly the ego's attempts to emulate its ideal rarely result in a copy that is even recognizable as such.

The perfect uniformity of mass produced consumer goods stands in a relation of utter indifference to contemporary human behaviour which is increasingly non-standard and marked by a sense of profound failure even when it comes to the desire to conform: to reproduce 'traditional family values' for example. The disconnection or gap between the *simulacrum* and its source or origin is filled in by nostalgia. This nostalgia occupies the same empty terrain that theory might occupy and sometimes prevents theory from entering. Here we would like to suggest that the interesting theoretical relationship is not between the *simulacrum* and the truth or authenticity that is thought to disappear at the moment of simulation. It is the contrast or difference between the absolute uniformity of *simulacra* and the absolute difference of human action that give the *simulacrum* its power and function in the postmodern world.

Increasingly, it is the *sameness* that now inhabits the former site of uniqueness, the sameness embodied in prestige mass produced consumer goods that is the only common point of desire in the postmodern world. Postmodernities as a matter of principle exhibit freedom of gender preference, and pray to different gods, but they all desire to drive a 500 Series Mercedes Benz or one of its good copies. That sameness is the reassurance postmodernites have that they are members of a primary group, that they have 'values in common' and share libidinal impulses. Particular commodities, scrupulously reproduced so each one is exactly the same as the others, have become ego ideals. Masses of consumers strive toward possession of these things and in so doing become the same in their egos. This may be the only thing they have in common, but it is very touchy and it can and does provide for intimacy based on narcissistic overflow in common into the same objects.[3] Far from marking the 'death of the social' as Baudrillard has suggested, mass consumption of industrially produced *simulacra* constitutes a return of some very primitive forms of sociability including spirit possession and totemic intensification of affect.

Under the influence of desire for a particular prestigious commodity, a consumer may lose all inhibition, exhibiting the most base emotions of jealously, envy, greed, avarice, lust. Feelings that should not be expressed if it is another human being that is their object can be freely stated if it is a Porsche. Consumers of prestige commodities feel no need justify their acts. Their purchases are self-justifying or have a 'taken-for-granted' basis in deep group consensus. The new sports car arrives with a huge red bow tied around it. Of course. To question the meaning of the purchase, or its future impact on family relations or household economies would be to puncture the magic of the moment. The spell of prestige commodities is hypnotic and contagious. Significant price reductions cause panic buying. The herd of consumers is impulsive, irritable, and acts without premeditation. When they do not have the things they want, they may become morbidly oppressed by their obsessive desires and live entirely within a fantasy of fulfilment. The love which they might feel for human intimates is diverted to the desired commodity. This diversion is socially positive so long as the commodity holds everyone together as the object of common desire. In fact, it may become the basis for a purer kind of love. Rather than him lusting after her or vice versa, and all the potential for love to go wrong, they are more reliably bonded by their common desire not for each other but for the Thing. For such perfect beings, going for a ride together in the sports car with its convertible top down may be experienced as 'better than sex'.

Every characteristic that has been attributed to primitive groups can be rediscovered in groups of postmodern consumers that strive toward possession of the same prestigious commodity. Each and every individual, no matter how different they might be, comes to think and feel the same. They think that possession of the coveted, now magical, object (a Rolex watch, for example) will give them an aura of invincibility in their social affairs. In the grouping of consumers of the same good, no one can be better than they are. Ownership of the requisite object puts them in a relation of pure equality with the other owners of the same things and thereby affirms the most fundamental principles of justice, fair play and primitive democracy.

There is an infinite array of consumer castes each one internally organized around the principle of member equality but all of them together arranged hierarchically. For some, it is not ownership of a Rolex or Rolls Royce that produces a primitive grouping; perhaps it is just ownership of a *new* as opposed to a used car or watch. A working-class respondent of ours recently confessed that he would like, just once before he dies, to be able to buy a new car. And, of course, for some others it is ownership of a car *that runs* that distinguishes them from some of their fellows and makes them the equal of others. This is the secret of the democratic paradox: how can a civilization founded on the principle of human equality have the greatest inequality ever known? A Mexican woman we know who picks crops in the Central Valley of California remembers the first year she was able to buy warm winter coats for her children as marking the beginning of her realization that her residency in the United States was permanent.

The new sites of exploitation are still unnamed and unexamined by sociology and critical theory but socioeconomic classes endure. How can we explain it? True, some older forms of exploitation remain in production processes, especially in the kind of production that is now routinely exported to the third world for former peasants to do. But much serious production is now accomplished with the flip of a switch: e.g. the transfer of a sequence of instructions into a floppy disk sold as a software package. The labour demands of postmodern production are not sufficient to explain the recrudescence of hierarchy in postmodernity. It is the unnoticed wandering of exploitation away from the sweatshops, not the absence of class, that is the reason postmodern theory tries to sidestep the question of class with its dramatic pronouncements: 'we now live in a post-scarcity society', the 'grand narrative of class is dead', etc.

THE NEW SITES OF EXPLOITATION

In the postmodern world, commodity *production* is no longer necessarily the site of exploitation. The reproduction of *simulacra* (e.g. pre-recorded video tapes, computer software packages, etc.) can be organized in such a way as to be low-energy consuming, clean and otherwise environmentally sustainable, and either labour free, or providing a reasonable return to labour. Statistically, the individual's relation to production is no longer a place on the assembly line, or in the mine, but a 'niche' in a transnational or global bureaucracy, a pastel little office or cubicle with a potted plant and a computer terminal. 'Work' and 'labour' in these niches increasingly resemble little dramas of work, or work masquerades, everyone costumed for their part, their looking 'professional' or 'seriously engaged', or even 'presidential', as important as any other aspect of their job 'performance'. The manufacture of *simulacra* becomes a prettified *simulacrum* of manufacture. We agree with Baudrillard that work environments transformed in this way do not sustain industrial class structures.

The production of *simulacra* appears as something that 'just happens' in the clean and cool 'work environments' of global corporations. But there is a missing element here. In order to reproduce *simulacra* it is necessary to have a *code* that acts as a set of instructions assuring repetition of the same form or structure. These *codes* are not the same as the commodities that are based on them. The instructions on the magnetic disk in our computers that allow us to manipulate a text took hundreds of work-years to create. Once created they can reproduce themselves effortlessly and endlessly.

Thus in the postmodern world, there are three potential sites of worker exploitation:

(1) The old industrial sites as first described by Marx and Engels where unimaginably hard work is demanded for minuscule reward in comparison to the amount of wealth it creates. This old industrial form of exploitation still exists in the work places recently exported to the third world and vice versa through the new migrations: for example, the 'clean rooms' of silicon valleys everywhere, in which women who assemble computer chips are literally bathed in toxic chemicals and suffer inordinately higher cancer rates and cannot carry their babies to term; in the chemically fertilized valleys of industrial agriculture.

(2) The new corporate sites that house 'service employees' at all levels which mainly exploit the emotional needs of their personnel for some kind of attachment. These are the sites that extract labour using an 'office-as-family' ideology, promising their workers something more than work. Specifically, they provide a group of intimates for whom one can dress up every day, enter into intrigues called 'office politics', act out fantasies ('office romances'), etc.[4] In short, they are set up to extract work in exchange not just for wages, but also for conferring an identity, self, or interesting persona, even a 'character', onto the worker. Great attention is paid to decor and image, landscaping, exercise rooms, etc. to attract workers who apparently feel that they could not otherwise afford the apparatus needed to construct what they would consider to be as good a version of themselves as the one they can get from the corporate environment.

(3) The sites where the *codes* are created in the first place. This third site is the frontier of corporate profits in a world organized around the exchange of *simulacra*. It is, therefore, strategically hidden and shifted. Few of the sites that are now organized under

the injunction, 'CREATE CODES THAT CAN BE USED FOR THE PRODUCTION OF SIMULACRA' can be linked directly to organized capital. The situation of the creators of computer software who work for large corporations is not necessarily typical. There are some who take oaths of secrecy and are bound by gag rules for years after their employment termination, who are required to sleep at their place of work during periods of rapid development and refinement of programs, etc. But this way of organizing the work of code creation retains an industrial style going back to the nineteenth-century practice of making the children who worked in the steel mills of Manchester sleep on straw pallets next to the blast furnaces. It is the genius and enormous good fortune of late capitalism to be able to externalize most of the costs of code creation on which production of *simulacra* depends and to detach itself from responsibility. New sites of exploitation include the *houses* and *garages* of editors, programmers, entertainers (and others) that have been transformed into places of work, where work never ends. Or, it can be the ghetto street habitat of gang members assuaging real pain with imaginative expressions of personal style that are immediately taken up as the code for next year's line of Guess Jeans and casual sportwear, *simulacra* of a hip hop urban existence, the ultimate achievement of which is to become a fad among the very groups that created the style in the first place so they must literally beg, borrow, and steal to buy back corporate copies of the life that has been taken from them.[5] Or, it can be the entire life of the woman who has adapted herself to modern professional existence and the special contingencies of that life for her sex. She may have made herself into a little production company to facilitate the shifting of roles from being 'daddy's little girl' for her husband, a tough customer to the service people who would like to sabotage her efforts, a friend who is 'not afraid to show her vulnerability', a protective maternal presence for her children, a merely competent non-threatening professional for her boss, a confidante to her dad. Every detail of her adaptation, every change of attitude, phrasing, costume and cosmetics that permits her to 'come off' as effectively feminine, maternal, domestic, and professional will be exploited as code, simulated and sold back to her.

MICKEY MOUSE AND THE NEW TECHNIQUES FOR COVERING THE SITE OF EXPLOITATION

When we re-read Baudrillard in preparation for writing this paper, we watched for a reflection on the figure of Mickey Mouse. We assumed a Baudrillard/Mickey encounter to be causally overdetermined. First, after Adorno's famous disagreement with Benjamin on the political meaning of audience responses to Mickey Mouse films for the future of fascism, Mickey became a standard topic of critical theory.[6] Baudrillard might have commented on Mickey just to support or correct existing scholarship. Second, given his interest in things American and Disney in particular, Baudrillard might have addressed the mouse that has become America's most internationally popular (corporate) cultural figure. Often he mentions Disneyland, ironically calling it 'paradise' and 'pure baroque logic' (1988: 98, 100). And he repeats as truth the romour that Walt Disney ordered his body to be cryogencially preseveed just before death to be thawed and treated when science finds a cure for the cancer that killed him.[7] But we could find no direct mention of Mickey. Third, the animated cartoon in general, and the figure of Mickey Mouse in particular, are virtually perfect examples of *simulacra* as theoretically given by Baudrillard. In Baudrillard's own terms, it can be said, perhaps only of Mickey Mouse and not of the examples Baudrillard himself provides, that Mickey is a

> . . . model of the real without origin or reality . . . This representational imaginary . . . is nuclear and genetic and no longer specular and discursive. With it goes all of metaphysics. No more mirror of being and appearances, of the real and its concepts; no more imaginary coextensivity: rather genetic miniaturization is the dimension of simulation.
>
> (From *Simulacra and Simulations* as reprinted in Poster 1988: 166–7)

We think that Mickey Mouse has never been so precisely conjured by critical theory, nor more pointedly ignored. What is at the base of this triple mystery? It is certainly not any reticence on Baudrillard's part to use something like a cartoon mouse in evidentiary support of his theoretical ideas.

Is Baudrillard afraid of the mouse? There is at least one *in*direct reference to Mickey in which Baudrillard confesses, '[t]he whole Walt Disney philosophy eats out of your hand with these pretty little sentimental creatures in grey fur coats. For my own part, I believe that behind these smiling eyes there lurks a cold, ferocious beast fearfully stalking us . . .' (1988: 48. Ellipses in the original). It is time to confront this celluloid/theoretical 'beast' onto which Baudrillard so readily projects his own fears.

The primary task of Mickey Mouse, in his role as the totemic animal of transnational corporate capitalist culture, guardian spirit of the 'Disney Empire', is to cover up the site of postmodern exploitation, the third form of exploitation, not the most crucial one: i.e., the site of alienated creativity, more specifically the creation of codes that are, in turn, stolen and used to generate endless series of *simulacra*. The technique of coverup is the by now standard one of hiding out in the open. As a double figure of creativity and repetition, of art and unchanging moral simple mindedness, Mickey Mouse articulates the pretence that a universal code has already been created. Why would corporate capitalism need to steal your life from you? It already has the model for the creation of the universal subject. It doesn't need your creativity. And the Mouse is everywhere as proof of this, in France even. There is no need to guard our complex cultural adaptations for what they are as precious contributions to the future of humanity. It is all universal by now.

Mickey succeeded by over-acting his part. He tried to be more than 'Everyman'. He tried to be the very symbol of 'universal*ism*' or perhaps 'universal*ity bitsy*'. He wanders freely in every class setting, in the homes of millionaires and in hovels, as if class does not matter. Like any leader, he made sacrifices. Somehow he knew, or someone knew, that he could function as a site of universal identification only to the extent that he gracefully embodied the powerlessness and abjection of the modern subject. In his drive to be universal he was represented as pure *lack* and made it his mission to make lack cute: he appeared without perspective, genderless, raceless, ageless. He had a squeaky little man-girl voice and was not easily distinguishable from Minnie. His toon forebears, Steamboat Willie, Felix the Cat, and Oswald the Lucky Rabbit were obviously black, but we can't tell about Mickey.[8] He bore the unshakably fecal aspect of his rodent status with dignity and good humour.[9] Only his trademark ears, which are certainly not ears, but much more faithful representations of breasts, testicles, or turds, could be called a physical defect serious enough to prompt suggestions of the need for cosmetic surgery should they occur in the human world.

But we are supposed politely to disattend these ears, pretend not to notice them, or even try to make him feel good about himself by volunteering for the same stigma, by putting on similar ears in deference to his condition. And, for his part, Mickey shows not the slightest sign of humiliation because of his ears. All this avoidance and normalization behaviour suggests the ears may actually represent the sexual parts lost as a condition of full participation in postmodernity where even presidents and kings are expected periodically to declare that they have no real power.

CONCLUSION

We are suggesting that Baudrillard took his analysis of the *simulacrum* up to the site of the new forms of capitalist exploitation that have introjected class structure into postmodernity. But he did not name the new sites of exploitation or initiate critical examination of them. His failure in this regard places his work at great risk. Historically it may contribute as much to the new forms of exploitation and their cover-up as to their exposure and eventual overthrow. He cannot 'read' or 'see' Mickey Mouse because Mickey stands in precisely the same relation to code creation as Baudrillard's theory taken in its entirety. Ultimately, both Baudrillard and Mickey Mouse insist on a generalized sense of the possible existence not of *codes*, which would be subversive, but of The Code, a single framework, already in existence, for everything. The Code, and correlatively the pretence of the absence of need for any new code, is the only field for the putative free play of *simulacra*, or the appearance of a figure of *lack* which can be universally worshipped. If there were *a* code, it truly would accommodate human life to the impossible, to death, to ultimate pleasure, to the real. If there were *a* code it would be equally and freely available to all human beings. Group, class, status, category, would disappear or be rendered insignificant. No wonder it is fervently desired by the prematurely utopian adherents of every political position. It would be stable and open to all for all time until the radical end of time that is supposed to be the Last Judgement.

Postmodernity affirms the possibility of The Code in the form of pure repetition, the *simulacrum*, and the 'random cannibalization of styles of the past', as Jameson put it. But postmodern capitalism is also committed to *apparent diversity* of consumer goods within the framework of a single Code, a commitment that produces a certain tension if not a contradiction and dialectic. Apparent diversity is achieved by the marketing of diverse codes the source and origin of which are officially unrecognized and repressed.

We suggest that what is being exploited by postmodern capitalism are the codes of those in the starkest of human situations, who have confronted 'the worst' most radically in their 'lifestyles' (= codes) or modes of relating to death and fulfilment. What is most successfully 'marketed' today are *simulacra* of whole ways of existing, adaptations of 'gang youth', punks, 'primitive' Brazilian Indians (*At Play in the Fields of the Lord*), homeless people, bag ladies, hookers, war victims, AIDS sufferers (the list is extended daily), their codes, the means they have worked out for dealing with the worst. We further suggest that Lacan was correct in his assertion that the 'panic' of the drive has displaced the Symbolic of desire for the contemporary or postmodern subject. There is no more 'needs fulfilment' in postmodernity. Capitalism, driven beyond its capacity to provide, has seen to that. All that it can promise us now is an endless series of futile attempts to accommodate that which cannot be accommodated: the satisfied need, ultimate *jouissance*, death. Its radical failure of symbolization leaves its believers 'eyeball to eyeball' with The Real. Postmodern capitalism is the realm of 'enjoyment', where the human subject is commanded 'to enjoy' but cannot, where pleasure that cannot be experienced spills over into The Thing, where our 'things' obscenely and menacingly enjoy themselves at our expense.

But there are those among us who deal directly with the absoluteness of loss, those who know there is no substitutability, no iterability, no supplement. They have carved out an existence on the empty gound between the possibility of the symbolization of desire and the dream of a single Symbolic-Paternal Order. They are the only possible source of a critical viewpoint on postmodern capitalism *and* of the creative energy needed to move it. We are disappointed with Baudrillard for not having found the site of postmodern exploitation, for giving us instead nostalgia for the medieval Church in the form of the now commonplace postmodern assertion of its absence. But if Baudrillard spends all his time with commodities-as-*simulacra*, with God as *simulacrum*, with things that can have no relation to need, there must be a reason for it. He is avoiding the ground that has been departed by the cause of desire, the ground where new codes are created as a matter of necessity. This is the reason he did not find Mickey Mouse. Mickey is there on the ground of departed desire as a defender of its borders, to block those who have not entered and to cover up the creative adaptations of those who have. Mickey permits us to imagine that there is a universal code of which he is the emanation and emissary, while his owners, if not his animators, know there are as many codes – ripe for the plucking – as there are human groupings. What Mickey does not permit us to imagine is *his* code: that his head, with the two ears that never change their location or position, that his head is not only the maternal breast and the castrated balls, but a motion picture projector. What this Mickey-projector reproduces is not a universal code for iteration as has been claimed. It is rather a faithful reproduction of the absolute loss human life is based upon; of the theft of its creativity, its reduction, and abject resignation in the face of The Real.

NOTES

The authors wish to thank Mark Calkins, Marilu Carter, and Elizabeth Freelund for their assistance with research on Disney and Mickey Mouse.

1 On the question of the persistence of class in postmodernity, we think that Roland Barthes' interpretation is still the best. See his 'Myth Today', especially pp. 140–41:

> Petit-bourgeois norms are the residues of bourgeois culture, they are bourgeois truths which have become degraded, impoverished, commercialized, slightly archaic, or shall we say, out of date? The political alliance of the bourgeoisie and the petite bourgeoisie has for more than a century determined the history of France; it has rarely been broken, and each time only temporarily (1848, 1871, 1936). This alliance got closer as time passed, it gradually became a symbiosis; transient awakenings that might happen, but the common ideology was never questioned again. The same 'natural' varnish covers up all 'national' representations: the big wedding of the bourgeoisie, which originates in a class ritual (the display and consumption of wealth), can bear no relation to the economic status of the lower middle class: but through the press, the news, and literature, it slowly becomes the very norm as dreamed, though not actually lived, of the petit bourgeois couple. The bourgeoisie is constantly absorbing into its ideology a whole section of humanity which does not have its basic status and cannot live up to it except in imagination, that is, at the cost of an immobilization and impoverishment of consciousness.

We will argue below that it is precisely through the *simulacrum* (of sumptuous weddings, etc.) that the stigmatized classes can come to believe that they have lived up to the bourgeois norm.

2 Note that often it is the absence of additional marking on the

commodity for which the consumer pays most dearly. Ferraris (and even Alfa Romeos) that had five-speed transmissions and fuel injected engines for twenty years have never blazoned 'Five Speed' or 'Fuel Injected' in chrome on the outside of the car. Only Chevrolets, Nissans and other mass-produced makes carry such markings. Thus the 'Five Speed' badge which wants to suggest a somewhat elevated status for the car also signifies that the car is of a type that cannot be assumed to be equipped with advanced technologies. So the consumer pays more not to have the mark and the consumer pays more to have the mark and in both cases the consumer pays precisely to be inscribed in a hierarchical system of classification.

3 Here it may be necessary to re-interpret the common practice of 'striping' one's Rolls Royce or Mercedes, including having one's name or initials 'tastefully' painted on the door. Within the framework of the interpretation being provided here, this practice may not ultimately be motivated by a desire to 'individualize' the car, to mark it off from the other Rolls's in the parking lot. It may be the opposite: not to indicate that the car belongs to me but rather that I belong to the car; not that I possess it, which would demean it, but that it is my ego ideal, that it has possessed me.

4 An unwanted byproduct of emotionalizing the work environment as a *simulacrum* of a nostalgic version of earlier domestic arrangements, the new 'extended family', has been the eruption of bloody violence between corporate co-workers stemming from long-simmering jealousies or love relations gone bad. Recently, the most violent murders in California, starting with the airline employee who put a gun to the head of a friend and co-worker who was piloting a crowded commuter plane, forcing him to fly straight down into the earth near Santa Barbara, killing everyone, have been of this type.

5 In Philadelphia today, black street gangs now identify themselves with particular lines of sports wear, the 'Adidas Gang' etc., which they wear to the exclusion of the other lines worn by their enemies.

6 See Adorno's (1973: 66) 18 March 1936 letter to Benjamin from London in which he remarks, in part, 'but if you take Mickey Mouse instead, things are far more complicated . . .'. For a discussion of the Adorno–Benjamin debate over the meaning of Mickey, and more recent contributions to Mickey Mouse theory (e.g. Stephen Jay Gould's) see Rickels (1991: 51–3, 61–4).

7 See *Simulacra and Simulation*, in Poster (1988: 171). Mark Calkins has reported to us that Disneyland Park employees are told that Walt Disney was buried according to normal procedures in his home town and that the 'on ice' story is only a myth.

8 Here we are indebted to a helpful unpublished paper by Marilu Correll Carter, 'Mickey Mouse's immaculate conception', Department of Applied Behavioral Sciences, University of California at Davis, 1991.

9 Not entirely. There was a symptomatic series of Sunday newspaper episodes in the 1930s in which Mickey repeatedly contemplated and attempted suicide. Interestingly the suicide attempts were the result of

unusual direct intervention from Walt Disney. Disney never wrote or drew the cartoon himself and apparently did not even monitor it much after the first few months of production. Floyd Gottfredson anonymously wrote and drew the strip from 1930 to 1975 after Ubbee Iwerks established Mickey's iconic form in 1929. In a 1975 interview, in response to a question about Walt Disney's involvement in producing the strip, Gottfredson comments:

> He would make suggestions every once in awhile, for some short continuities and so on, and I would do them. One that I will never forget, and which I still don't understand – around early 1931 I believe it was, he said, 'Why don't you do a continuity of Mickey trying to commit suicide?' So I said 'Walt! You're kidding!' He replied, 'No, I'm not kidding. I think you could get a lot of funny stuff out of that.' . . . So I did, oh, maybe ten days of Mickey trying to commit suicide – jumping off bridges and landing in garbage scows, trying to hang himself and the limb breaks . . . [S]trangely enough the Syndicate didn't object. We didn't hear anything from the editors, and Walt said, 'See, it was funny; I told you.'

(Hamilton 1988: 107–8)

REFERENCES

Adorno, Theodor (1973) 'Letters to Walter Benjamin', *New Left Review* 81, September–October, 55–82.

Barthes, Roland (1972) *Mythologies*, New York, Hill and Wang.

Baudrillard, Jean (1975) *The Mirror of Production*, St. Louis, Telos Press.

—— (1976) *L'Echange symbolique et la mort*, Paris, Gallimard.

—— (1981) *For a Critique of the Political Economy of the Sign*, St. Louis, Telos Press.

—— (1988) *America*, London and New York, Verso.

—— (1990) *Cool Memories*, London and New York, Verso.

Benjamin, Walter (1969) *Illuminations*, ed. Hannah Arendt, New York, Schocken.

Eco, Umberto (1986) *Travels in Hyperreality*, New York, Harcourt Brace Jovanovich.

Hamilton, Bruce (ed.) (1988) *Walt Disney's Mickey Mouse in Color*, New York, Pantheon.

Kellner, Douglas (1989) *Jean Baudrillard: From Marxism to Postmodernism and Beyond*, Palo Alto, Stanford.

Poster, Mark (ed.) (1988) *Jean Baudrillard: Selected Writings*, Palo Alto, Stanford.

Rickels, Laurence A. (1991) *The Case of California*, Baltimore and London, Johns Hopkins.

Chapter 8

Cruising America

Bryan S. Turner

> At dawn my bus was zooming across the Arizona desert – Indio,
> Blythe, Salome (where she danced); the great dry stretches lead-
> ing to Mexican mountains in the south. Then we swung north to
> the Arizona mountains, Flagstaff, cliff-towns. I had a book with
> me I stole from a Hollywood stall, *Le Grand Meaulnes* by Alain-
> Fournier, but I preferred reading the American landscape as we
> went along. Every bump, rise, and stretch in it mystified my
> longing.
>
> Jack Kerouac, *On the Road*

Rainer Maria Rilke in a 'well-known letter' (de Man 1989: 30) com-
plained about the inauthentication of modern culture under the
impact of technology, especially with the penetration of American
technological values:

> From America have come to us now empty, indifferent things,
> artificial things that deceive us by simulating life . . . In the
> American sense, a house or an apple tree or a grapevine has
> nothing in common with the house, the fruit, or the grape in
> which our ancestors have invested their hopes and cares.
>
> (Rilke 1950: 898–9)

Heidegger quotes the letter in *Poetry, Language, Thought*
(Heidegger 1971: 113) as an illustration for his criticism of modern
nihilism, following Neitzsche, in which the quest for world mastery
in the form of the will to power was turned negatively against itself,
becoming a blind urge to will (Stauth and Turner 1988a). Thus, the
association between technological mastery, the levelling impact of
democracy, the commodification of all values by capitalism and
Americanism was a typical component of conservative romanticism

in Germany at the end of the nineteenth century. America was seen to have undermined the traditional values and practices of German civilization, and created a simulated world of false values. America combined a democratic polity which flattened social values behind the 'herd', as Nietzsche had called the democratic mass, with a technologically advanced capitalism, which standardized life by making technical trinkets available to a consumer market. Nietzsche had seen the French Revolution in terms of a set of contrasts between equality and individuality, mass culture and personal creativity; in this respect Nietzsche's critique of Rousseau was similar to the general consensus of the French educated elite (Ansell-Pearson 1991: 32–3).

The anti-American accent to German conservatism was central to the early Heidegger's critique of the instrumental reason of modern capitalism. This sentiment is very obvious in *The Question Concerning Technology* (Heidegger 1977) and in his *Introduction to Metaphysics* (Heidegger 1959: 37–8) where Heidegger made a famous comparison of Russia and America:

> This Europe, which in its ruinous blindness is forever on the point of cutting its own throat, lies today in a great pincers, squeezed between Russia on the one hand and America on the other. From a metaphysical point of view, Russia and America are the same: the same dreary technological frenzy, the same unrestricted organization of the average man.

It was this 'dreary technological frenzy' which had created a global order in which trivial news could be consumed instantly, which had destroyed time and which had produced a culture where 'a boxer is regarded as a nation's great man'. Heidegger went on to argue, of course, that it was the task of Germany, caught between these two technological giants, to assert once more the great spiritual values of European culture. More precisely, Heidegger welcomed the triumph of Hitler as the triumph of authenticity over the abstract universalism of democratic rights. In fact, in a conversation with Karl Jaspers which is recalled in Jaspers's *Philosophische Autobiographie*, Heidegger protested that Hitler's lack of education and culture were insignificant considered against the beauty and power of Hitler's hands. It was the charismatic authenticity of Hitler's body which was at issue, not vague principles about legitimacy and democracy (Wolin 1990: 106).

The ambiguity towards American capitalist mass democracy was further complicated by racist attitudes towards black American soldiers in Germany in the interwar and war years. The fascist concern for health and racial purity demanded a strong eugenics programme to guarantee the future health of the population. It has been estimated that one percent of the German population was legally sterilized between 1934 and 1945 in the interests of racial purity, and a large group of gypsies, mulattos and Jews were illegally sterlized. These practices were further intensified by the SS under the regime of Nazi medicine. The fact that America was a migrant settler society with considerable ethnic diversity thus confirmed the conservative fears that Americanization would always entail a genetic corruption. Military defeat in the first world war had brought black French African troops onto German soil, creating a sexual panic among racial purists (Theweleit 1987: 94). Military defeat in the second world war had the same consequences. Throughout this period America's relatively open immigration policy meant that the United States, from the perspective of European racism, was a genetic dumping ground.

The important feature of the conservative critique of American materialism and cultural vulgarity by German intellectuals was that it was reiterated throughout Europe by radical left-wing writers. The crass materialism of the 'culture industry' was a favourite topic of Frankfurt School radicals; it was the very foundation of Adorno's views on jazz, film and mass culture (Adorno 1991). Of course, given the fact that the Frankfurt School tradition was primarily Jewish, one cannot criticize left-wing intellectuals of racism, but they have often shared a common hostility to American cultural deprivation with right-wing conservatives. The critical theorists' search for a genuine life-world which is free from 'cultural impoverishment' involves a nostalgic quest for real cultural values, and it is often difficult to separate this perspective from conservative complaints about cultural inauthentication in a rational society (Stauth and Turner 1988b).

Where Heidegger has been a source of inspiration for contemporary writers on the political Left, one can find yet again this equation of American culture and technological capitalism with the negative consquences of mass consumerism. Luc Ferry and Alain Renaut (1990: 86) are justified in complaining, with reference to Heidegger's *Introduction to Metaphysics*, 'What we need to understand now is how a translation of this passage into the language of today may provide virtually intact, for an important segment of the leftist intelligentsia yearning for Marxism, the necessary resuscitating of the defunct figure of the critical intellectual.' The romantic anti-industrial criticism of capitalism, in which one would include figures like Georg Lukács, and the Heideggerian critique of instrumental rationalism tend to merge into a common opposition to the alleged falsification of life by American capitalist culture.

French radical intellectuals have probably been no less anti-American than their German counterparts. Given the influence of existentialism and Marxism on post-war French intellectuals, it is hardly surprising that writers like Raymond Aron were treated with such contempt. Many of these issues were addressed by Aron in *The Opium of the Intellectuals* (Aron 1962). French intellectuals aspired to an autonomous Europe, wherein they would exercise a central cultural and political role; this aspiration was the source of their anti-Americanism (Colquhoun 1986). Furthermore, America was relatively successful as a materialistic democracy and its success had depended on competition, private finance, market forces and a decentralized political system. American success could not be explained by the methods which the Left favoured, namely, state intervention, corporatist politics and collectivist values. America had not achieved global dominance through direct imperialism and colonalism, as traditional imperial powers like France and Britain had. Finally, American democratic culture was overtly anti-intellectual, and as a result America became the most obvious target of left-wing European wrath (Hollander 1992).

However, one major difference between German and French political culture is that the revolutionary political history of France is inextricably bound up with the revolutionary tradition of democratic America. It is in this context that Alexis de Tocqueville's *Democracy in America* is of such central cultural importance to the dialogue between Europe and North America. De Tocqueville's study of the institutions of the new American democracy appeared in two sections in 1835 and 1840. It was based on a double subterfuge. First, de Tocqueville, who went ostensibly to report on American penal institutions, used his journey to explore his own interests in political institutions, and second, the book is not really about America but about democracy itself. It was a study of the most profound political revolution in modern history, namely, the triumph of the expectation of egalitarianism, but the book's impact probably lay more in de Tocqueville's ambiguities about democracy, especially the impact of a mass democracy on individual taste and discernment. The democratic revolution installed the principle of equality of condition at the heart of American institutions, but it was precisely that principle which threatened to undercut the culture of individualism, which was also an essential ingredient of American social and economic dynamism.

De Tocqueville's masterpiece was thus a great study in the tyranny of the masses, and it was received in Europe by writers like John Stuart Mill as a warning against the tyranny of majority opinion inside a reformed parliamentary system. The consequences of a mass democracy and mass culture for individual differences would prove to be disastrous. Following Wilhelm von Humboldt, Mill argued that 'variety of situations' was essential to individual cultivation. The spread of (American) democracy as a revolution in the equality of condition would result in a tyranny of mass opinion to which Mill referred as 'Chinese stationariness' (Turner 1974). The disappearance of differences of rank would produce a spiritual death:

> Formerly, different ranks, different neighbourhoods, different trades and professions, lived in what might be called different worlds; at present to a great degree in the same. Comparatively speaking, they now read the same things, go to the same places, have their hopes and fears directed to the same objects, have the same rights and liberties, and the same means of asserting them . . . The combination of all these causes forms so great a mass of influences hostile to Individuality, that it is not easy to see how it can stand its ground.

> (Mill 1962: 130–1)

There is again a connection with Nietzsche's critique of the mass, because Nietzsche came across de Tocqueville from his reading of Mill. For Nietzsche also, the American revolution had ushered in a new era, an era without God in which the new idol was the state. With the decline of Christianity, there was a great danger that the state would promote a false culture, suitable for the new class of bourgeois money-makers. This uniform social levelling would bring about an 'animalization of man' and a false individualism of sameness (Stauth and Turner 1988b: 107). As early as the 1840s, therefore, we can find European writers looking towards America as a source of revolutionary values which will undermine rank, distinction and hence individuality in the Old World. The idea behind Mill's anxious analysis and Nietzsche's bitter criticism was the thought that individual difference would be swallowed up in American mass society.

Baudrillard's *America* is self-consciously located within the context of this transatlantic critical tradition. Baudrillard is very aware of the legacy of transatlantic misunderstandings which have plagued analysis in the past and he warns American intellectuals not to cast 'a nostalgic eye towards Europe, its history, its metaphysics, its cuisine, and its past' (Baudrillard 1989: 79). The problem for America 'is the crisis of an achieved utopia, confronted with the problem of its duration and permanence' (p. 77). Hence, 'Equality is part of the way of life here' (p. 93). The problem for Europe is melancholy, the failure of its revolutionary ideals — democracy, freedom, reason. But these comparisons, of course, have a history. It is impossible for a French intellectual to write about America without the shadow of de Tocqueville shaping the analysis. Part of the history of this transatlantic discourse is the European view of American naivety, simplicity and, above all, scientific crassness. European phenomenology, hermeneutics, critical theory and deconstructionist techniques were all developed against a background of American positivism and pragmatism. The abstract theoreticism of European philosophy has been self-consciously elaborated not just as a criticism of positivism and empiricism in general, but as a critique of *American* positivism and empiricism. It is not possible to read Baudrillard's poetic fiction of *America* without this burden of transatlantic mystification. 'America' is always already constituted within political discourse as the idol of modern times.

There is no need here to analyse Baudrillard's study of America in detail. It has been done elsewhere (Gane 1991a; Kellner 1989; Vidich 1991) and by Barry Smart in this volume. By and large, the book has been either dismissed or received with a deal of criticism. Thus, Kellner (1989: 170) comments 'uncharitably, one could read the book as a whole as symptomatic of the decline of Baudrillard's theoretical powers and the collapse of social analysis and critique — as well as politics — in favor of highly uneven social observation and metaphysical ruminations'. Baudrillard has been seduced, according to Kellner, by the French cultural scene, and 'although he resisted mass media appearances for many years, when the media turned to him to celebrate his simulated confessions/notebooks, *Cool Memories*, he took to the broadcast waves for his fifteen minutes of media celebrity' (Kellner 1989: 151). Alex Callinicos

(1989: 147) was equally scathing, claiming that Baudrillard had adopted a 'version of the Myth of the Noble Savage', but with a reverse value-judgement that Europeans are merely powerless onlookers. Baudrillard's contrast between America and Europe 'remains stunningly banal' and Baudrillard's apologetics are based on the assumption that criticism is no longer possible.

What is the nature of the offence of *America* (Baudrillard 1989) and the autobiographical *Cool Memories* (Baudrillard 1990a)? One answer is to see *America* as an illustration of the impact of Situationist positions on Baudrillard's work (Plant 1992: 134–49). It appears to avoid any simplistic critique of American values, at least directly. The signs and images of the modern world of mass media represent no other, deeper, more important reality. They may sustain a belief in a representational reality, but they circumscribe the world rather than indicating it. The consequence is that 'things are simply as they appear to be' (Plant 1992: 134). Criticism is merely dissolved in this sign-mass, rather like cosmic matter disappearing into black holes. These ideas against criticism were, of course, established in Baudrillard's earlier work such as *In the Shadow of the Silent Majorities* (1983). While the masses are constantly questioned, interrogated, surveyed, analysed and measured, the masses are opaque to such measures which are based on antiquated ideas about representation. It is not that the masses are silent; 'it is a silence which *refuses to be spoken for in its name*' (Baudrillard 1983: 22). Conventional methods of enquiry are fatuous in the presence of this implosive reality.

In addition, *America* and *Cool Memories* are offensive to academics, especially serious academics like Callinicos and Kellner, because they are politically uncommitted, whimsical, and depthless. *Cool Memories* reads as a clever, but disconnected, set of notes on Baudrillard's personal experience of America. The parallel text of *America* appears to have more organization and is self-consciously designed as a text with an audience in mind. If we think about these two volumes from the point of view of their style, they are postmodern in the limited sense that they exhibit the characteristics of 'cruising'. A cruise is a trip or voyage typically undertaken for pleasure; it is a trivial exercise. The tourist on a cruise attracts a negative response from those who are local inhabitants, because, like Simmel's 'The Stranger', they are marginal and in that sense dangerous. The stranger (*der Fremde*) is detached and rootless, expressing a general human estrangement (*Entfremdung*) and a nostalgia for settlement and security. Cruising is pointless, aimless and unproductive. It leaves no residue, no evidence, no archive. It does not intend to interpret; it is post-anthropological. Baudrillard's postmodern cruising through American culture could be seen as a contemporary version of the 1960s genre novel of the car ride or the more traditional hobo's journey across America. It is for this reason that I have started this chapter with a quotation from Jack Kerouac's famous 1950s novel *On the Road* to suggest this link between a drop-out culture of the highway and the post-modern depthless ride through the American landscape. In his two novels, *The Town and the City* and *On the Road*, Kerouac articulated the Beat creed of 'dig everything' and integrated the worlds of the literati, hoodlums and junkies. For Kerouac, cool memories record the 'with-it' culture, the culture of the itinerant jazz musician. Baudrillard's 'cool memories' record a post-literate society where television and radio may destroy the traditional hierarchies of the 'hot' high culture. Furthermore, Kerouac's staccato sentences describing this quasi-criminal underworld of Beat poets provided a celebratory commentary on American sub-cultures. Both Baudrillard and Kerouac are involved in a 'reading' of the society through the flashing vision of American culture as a seen through the car screen, the rear mirror or the subway. The car screen and the TV screen have a number of things in common. The passenger, like the viewer, is passive, indifferent, entertained and perhaps over-stimulated by the flashing trivia of the landscape and the scene.

The postmodern argument about reading is that the experience of the TV screen is very different from the experience of the printed page of a book. The book is not simply the product of the print age; it requires a special type of discipline and seriousness which is not demanded by the largely passive experience of viewing the television (Gane 1991b: 49). The TV image is depthless, flickering, immaterial. Furthermore, one can instantly channel-hop from 'serious drama' to *Sesame Street*, from 'real' news to *Spitting Image.* The channel-hop is the uncommitted, random overview of a variety of options, to which the viewer/passenger is indifferent. The fragmentation of pop culture, the pastiche of manufactured cultures, the flickering movie image, the simulated Disney culture — these experiences of modern life are thought to induce exactly that distracted, rootless state of mind that is equivalent to the experience of endless and random channel-hopping (Hebdige 1986–7). As

Baudrillard (1989: 9) says, 'Driving is a spectacular form of amnesia. Everything is to be discovered, everything to be obliterated.'

Channel-hopping is par excellence the visual experience of cruising, but it is also moral cruising/The postmodern claim is that the TV experience is uncommitted. The couch potato, in experiencing everything visually, is involved in nothing in practice./The experience of car-cruising by strangers or tourists sampling a landscape is very similar. There is no metanarrative of the highway; postcards returned to base merely invite empathy for the ride ('Wish you were here'). Reading the car screen as tourist and *flâneur* is parallel to the channel-hopping viewer as voyeur. Depthlessness is brought about by cruising through the landscape. Reading through the car screen is a voyeuristic consumption of a series of signs, the detached and therefore cynical cruise through hyperreality. Travellers are the contemporary version of the Simmelian stranger – rootless and homeless, they are carriers of cultural nostalgia. Both *America* and *Cool Memories* capture this experience of flicking through a society, of cruising through a landscape, and of tourist sampling of cultures. Baudrillard's gaze appears equally cynical, detached, witty. By playing along the surface, it is a gaze which avoids the weight of scholarship – 'The point is not to write the sociology or psychology of the car, the point is to drive. That way you can learn more about this society than all academia could ever tell you' (Baudrillard 1989: 54).

The results of this flickering gaze exhibit a certain brilliance. Baudrillard can be admired and praised for capturing this postmodern experience of flâneurism through the production of a sociological fiction within the genre of the 'sentimental journey', of which the beat generation's car ride can be an example. Rather than condemning his apparent lack of theory, lack of commitment and lack of seriousness, we should try to read Baudrillard as a poetics of the screen image, as a modern de Tocqueville not on horseback, but as the Kerouacian poet from 'The Time of the Geek' who makes an 'unsentimental' journey through a landscape. The use of the desert – 'the most beautiful place I shall ever see' (Baudrillard 1990a: 3) – as location and metaphor is particularly powerful as an image of urban America. Thus, Baudrillard's own work itself reflects the world he is describing rather than analysing, dissecting and criticizing. Baudrillard's poetics closes the gap between theory and reality by shadowing or paralleling the American dream (Hebdige 1988).

When art historians want to indicate a certain self-conscious artistry, they talk about the 'painterly' qualities of a creative artist. For a sociologist (by trade at least), Baudrillard is extraordinarily 'writerly'. It is difficult to read *America* and *Cool Memories* without being conscious of their great style, reflexivity and writerly qualities. What are the ingredients of the Baudrillardian imagination of the highway? First, style, or form, is everything; content and matter are diversions. The celebratory form and self-consiousness of style are particularly prominent in the imaginary vision of 'astral America' (Baudrillard 1989: 27):

> Astral America. The lyrical nature of pure circulation . . . Sideration. Starblasted, horizontally by the car, altitudinally by the plane, geologically by deserts.

Secondly, the message is built up by repetition in a cumulative explosion of meaning:

> Anorexic culture: a culture of disgust, of expulsion, of anthropoemia, of rejection. Characteristic of a period of obesity, saturation, overabundance.
>
> (p. 39)

Thirdly, he achieves his effects by hyperbole, perhaps the literary equivalent of hyperreality, which achieves its goals by exaggeration beyond convention, common sense and/or custom. Hyperboles are constructed literary means to shock, but they are not to be taken literally. To take some examples,

> all the myths of modernity are American,

or

> the whole of America is a desert,

or

> there is no culture here.

Finally, neither *America* nor *Cool Memories* has to be read in any sequence. One can cruise through these volumes without regard for argumentation or presentation, because each phrase or sentence or paragraph appears to be self-sustaining and autonomous. Each unit is meaningful. It is aesthetically pleasing to channel-hop through Baudrillard's work, sampling the style, tasting the bon mot, admiring the wit, enjoying the topography of his imaginative journey, or being dazzled by the outrageous metaphors, but these experiences have nothing to do with reading an argument from premises to conclusions. It is for this reason that I have suggested a parallel between passively watching a pleasing television spectacular, watching a landscape shoot by from the detachment of a car window, or flicking through Baudrillard's exquisite prose. The spectacle of astral America is magically conjured up by the physical experience of travelling in a hot landscape – 'gliding down the freeway, smash hits on the Chrysler stereo, heat wave' (Baudrillard 1989: 1). Baudrillard's glittering sentences resemble the 'soundbites' of American commercial discourse; they are items of meaning flashing across a screen rather like the bill-boards which flash past our car screens. Meaning is broken up into digestible chunks.

While this interpretation of intellectual postmodern cruising as a parallel to tourism as cruising or life-style cruising appears to fit the vocabulary and overt purpose of *America*, there may be a better way of reading these volumes, namely as a twentieth-century version of La Rochefoucauld's seventeenth-century *Maximes et Mémoires*. La Rochefoucauld's maxims are also reflections (*Réflexions diverses*) which are constituted by aphorisms, proverbs, *pensées*, and apophthegms on life. *Cool Memories* are also aphoristic reflections, cool memories of a hot culture. One objection to this claim might be that La Rochefoucauld's reflections, rather like Montaigne's essays, were the product of aristocratic leisure, withdrawal from society and cultivated idleness. The audience of *America* is not an educated, land-owing aristocracy. While Baudrillard's audience is not a ritualized status group, it is a literate audience in a society which Baudrillard regards as post-literate and, increasingly, an educated class in an oral culture. Furthermore, one suspects that the last maxim of *Cool Memories* (Baudrillard 1990a: 234) is the most significant: 'This journal is a subtle matrix of idleness.'

Much analytical debate surrounds the maxim as a literary form, but basically the maxim condenses meaning into a shortened form in order to express some (moral) truth. However, in the maxim, we admire not only the brevity but the carefully constructed form in which meaning ultimately is submerged by the dexterity of its literary shell. By immobilizing meaning, the maxim eventually destroys it. Truth becomes a truism, because form subordinates content. When maxims are published as a collection, there is an immediate problem as to how they should be read, randomly or sequentially. The problem is that they have no necessary or intrinsic relationship to each other. Cruising becomes a necessity

> . . . for each blank space separating one maxim from the next interrupts the flow of thought before it picks up momentum, laying out an open dimension of time and space for reflection, for weighing the maxim just read, for returning to a *table rase* before reading the next one.

(Lewis 1977: 46)

Maxims are sound-bites of an unfinished moral code.

Although the collection of maxims appears therefore to have no necessary order, some critics have argued that the very fragmentation and discontinuity of the maxim as an art form reflected the precarious and fragmented nature of the baroque period. La Rochefoucauld's seemless web of maxims creates a sense of dizziness and emptiness, reflecting the emptiness of human life. This baroque anthropology was, indirectly through the chaos of the reflections, a critique of the conception of human nature in the classical world; the maxim is a critique of the metanarratives of the classical world. The disorder of the maxims thus provided a perfect simulation of the disorder of society.

I have already suggested in 'Baudrillard for sociologists' that there is a parallel between the postmodern critique of modernity and the baroque assault on Puritan capitalist modernity. Baudrillard himself frequently employs 'baroque' to describe modern society. Disneyland is an example of 'pure baroque logic' (Baudrillard 1989: 101); 'the Vietnam war never happened, perhaps it was only a dream, a baroque dream of napalm and the tropics' (1987: 17); 'with this melange of concepts and categories, as with the mixing and promiscuity of the races, one should imagine the baroque effects of transfiguration' (1990b: 58). It may be perfectly appropriate therefore to suggest a parallel between the baroque fascination for the disordered text of a collection of brilliant maxims, where each maxim eventually destroys truth by elevating form over content, and the construction and style of Baudrillard's cool memories. In particular, the precision and condensation of meaning in the maxim tends to render it meaningless. For example, Mme de Lafayette could not decide conclusively which of these maxims is true: either 'Unfaithfulness is pardoned, but it is not forgotten' or 'Unfaithfulness is forgotten, but it is not pardoned'.

Each is perfect in expressing the form of the maxim, but do they represent any human reality? The maxim threatens to slip constantly into meaninglessness, because its form often suggests the possibility of an inversion.⌋

The baroque fascination for the ruin, the construction of reality, the incompleteness of the world, the artifice and the artificial has much in common with our sense of the endlesslessly constructed and simulated, in Baudrillard's terminology, character of 'the social' in hyperreality. The collection of maxims can be seen as a ruin, a necessarily incomplete architecture of meaning. It is a ruin because it can never be wholly assembled, but it is also ruined because it is by definition random. I have suggested that Baudrillard's *America* can be read as a collection of baroque/postmodern maxims. Let us at random take some examples:

America is neither dream nor reality;

The desert is a sublime form that banishes all sociality, all sentimentality, all sexuality;

This is a world that has shown genius in its irrepressible development of equality, banality, and indifference.

Baudrillard's other works exhibit this same fascination with the aphorism. For example, from 'Figures of the Transpolitical in *Fatal Strategies* (Baudrillard 1990b: 55):

More visible than the visible – this is the obscene. More invisible than the invisible – this is the secret.

This claim about Baudrillard's argumentative dependence on the bon mot appears to be even more striking in the case of *Cool Memories*. Again a few examples will serve to make the point:

Dying is nothing. All you have to know is how to disappear;

The ultimate achievement is to live beyond the end, by any means whatever;

Culture contradicts all genetic capital;

A positive judgement gives you more satisfaction than praise, provided it smacks of jealousy.

Now rather like the baroque maxim, the meaningfulness of these postmodern aphorisms can be called into question by inversion. For example,

Living is everything. All you have to know is how to appear;

The ultimate end is to live beyond achievement, by any means whatever;

All genetic capital contradicts culture;

A positive judgement gives you more dissatisfaction than condemnation, provided it smacks of pure resentment.

Finally, consider the possibilities of obscenity:

More visible than the invisible – this is the (ob)scene.

CONCLUSION

European élite culture has for two centuries regarded America with a mixture of fear and superiority. American mass democracy and American mass culture have been interpreted as necessary components of an inferior capitalist system. The paradox of this cultural condemnation has been the convergence of left and right criticism. The Left condemned America as the leading capitalist system within which both democracy and culture were a sham. The Right condemned capitalism because it had disrupted the stable hierarchical values of traditional society, opening up the social system to the levelling of democracy and the falsity of mass culture.

This situation of radical criticism has been transformed by the collapse of organized communism in Eastern Europe and the Soviet Union, but this transformation has taken place alongside the erosion of American economic hegemony. Baudrillard's work has to be read in the context of post-Marxism, but also in the context of American decline: 'Today the orgy is over' (Baudrillard 1989: 107). Thus, Baudrillard's analysis of American decline has to be interpreted within a particular tradition of European critical analysis of America, but the important feature of his commentary is the avoidance of the condemnatory language of both the Left and the Right. For Baudrillard, America is utopia realized. He also recognizes that, while American economic power may have been undermined, its cultural dominance is now supreme. Because Americans are unable or at least reluctant to think about this economic decline, they live in a fantasy, Disney world – 'a sunny screen memory' (Baudrillard 1989: 108).

This fantasy land is not analysed by Baudrillard by the conventional means of sociology or political science. It is achieved stylistically, first of all by the literary convention of the journey, and secondly by what I have regarded as the device of the baroque memoir. The travel theme gives the text a perfect feeling of depthlessness, of skating over the surface. The maxim condenses this mood, by contrast, into the stylized phrase or sentence. Of these sentences we might, à la Baudrillard himself, say that they are completely memorable, wholly forgettable. But this observation should be taken as praise, because it is precisely this sense of fleeting reality which expresses the postmodern mood. In both politics and culture, the advertising agencies have also condensed reality into the maxim or the easily recalled image. In a period where international politics can be summarized for at least six million British citizens in a phrase like 'Up yours Delors!', when a former American vice-president, who believes that Latin is the official language of Latin America, can also ascribe a superfluous 'e' to the humble potato, or when an entire country can be persuaded that its national water supply can be sold off to private individuals as a commodity, Baudrillard is probably correct to declare that 'We are all hostages now' (1990b: 35).

You know it makes sense.

REFERENCES

Adorno, T. (1991) *The Culture Industry*, London, Routledge.
Ansell-Pearson, K. (1991) *Nietzsche contra Rousseau. A Study of Nietzsche's Moral and Political Thought*, Cambridge, Cambridge University Press.
Aron, R. (1962) *The Opium of the Intellectuals*, New York, Norton.
Baudrillard, J. (1983) *In the Shadow of the Silent Majorities*, New York, Semiotext(e).
—— (1987) *The Evil Demon of Images*, Sydney, The Power Institute.
—— (1989) *America*, London, Verso.
—— (1990a) *Cool Memories*, London, Verso.
—— (1990b) *Fatal Strategies*, New York, Semiotext(e).
Callinicos, A. (1989) *Against Postmodernism. A Marxist Critique*, Cambridge, Polity Press.
Colquhoun, R. (1986) *Raymond Aron*, London, Sage, 2 volumes.
de Man, P. (1989) *Critical Writings 1953–1978*, Minneapolis, University of Minnesota Press.

Ferry, L. and Renaut, A. (1990) *Heidegger and Modernity*, Chicago and London, University of Chicago Press.

Gane, M. (1991a) *Baudrillard. Critical and Fatal Theory*, London, Routledge.

—— (1991b) *Baudrillard's Bestiary*, London, Routledge.

Hebdige, D. (1986–7) 'A report on the Western Front: Postmodernism and the "politics" of style', *Block* 12, 4–26.

—— (1988) *Hiding in the Light: On Images and Things*, London, Comedia.

Heidegger, M. (1959) *Introduction to Metaphysics*, New Haven, Yale University Press.

—— (1971) *Poetry, Language, Thought*, New York, Harper & Row.

—— (1977) *The Question Concerning Technology and Other Essays*, New York, Harper & Row.

Hollander, P. (1992) *Anti-Americanism. Critiques at Home and Abroad 1965–1990*, Oxford, Oxford University Press.

Kellner, D. (1989) *Jean Baudrillard. From Marxism to Postmodernism and Beyond*, Cambridge, Polity Press.

Lewis, P. E. (1977) *La Rochefoucauld. The Art of Abstraction*, Ithaca and London, Cornell University Press.

Mill, J. S. (1962) *Utilitarianism, Liberty and Representative Government*, London, J.M. Dent.

Plant, S. (1992) *The Most Radical Gesture. The Situationist International in a Postmodern Age*, London, Routledge.

Stauth, G. and Turner, B. S. (1988a) 'Nostalgia, postmodernism and the critique of mass culture', *Theory, Culture and Society* 5(2–3), 509–26.

—— (1988b) *Nietzsche's Dance. Resentment, Reciprocity and Resistance in Social Life*, Oxford, Basil Blackwell.

Theweleit, K. (1987) *Male Fantasies*, Oxford, Basil Blackwell, 2 volumes.

Turner, B. S. (1974) 'The concept of social "stationariness": utilitarianism and Marxism', *Science & Society* 38(1), 1–19.

Vidich, A. J. (1991) 'Baudrillard's *America*', *Theory, Culture and Society*, 8(2), 135–44.

Wolin, R. (1990) *The Politics of Being. The Political Thought of Martin Heidegger*, New York, Columbia University Press.

Name index

Subject index

abstaining 29
Academy, the ix–x, xv, 74, 85;
  institutional closure in xv,
  xvii n.8
addictive substances 9
advertising 2, 4, 117
affluence, disease of 11
AIDS xii, 39, 133, 142
America ix, x, xii, xiv, 47, 48,
  50–1, 52–3, 54–5, 56–60,
  62–4, 65–6, 72, 109, 110,
  119–20, 139, 146–8, 149–50,
  151–6, 158–60; Astral 155, 156;
  Baudrillard and Eco on x; and
  the desert 56; and Europe 47,
  48–51, 52, 53, 54, 57–60,
  61–2, 63, 65, 66, 148, 151–2,
  159; and immigration 148;
  Indian discoverers of 50; and
  the real 59; and realism 53
America (Baudrillard) x, xvii n.7,
  57–60, 62, 64, 66, 74, 75, 85,
  119–20, 151, 152, 154, 155,
  156, 158
Amerika (Kafka) 75
American: Century 65; culture 56,
  62–3, 75, 79–80, 148, 155, 159;
  Dream 63, 154; hegemony 47,
  65; hyperreality x, 53, 62;
  imagination 53; military strategy
  54, 64; modernity 54, 58, 64,
  66; Revolution 58, 150
anomaly 115
anomie 115
Apocalypse Now (Coppola) 116

appearance 89–90, 92, 93, 96,
  103, 104, 159; *see also*
  disappearance
architecture, postmodern 60, 71
Asia 48–9
authenticity 107, 134
automaton 100
A-world 32, 33, 34, 35, 36, 37, 38,
  40; and Sherlock Holmes 35; *see
  also* B-World

Baroque culture 83–4
being xii, 34
beings 32–3, 34
bit(s), electronic 97, 99, 102
black soldiers in Germany 148
black street gangs 144 n.5
bodies 122 n.2; global circulation
  of 120; of the nobility 26;
  suspect 26; women and their 92
body, the xiv, 5, 7, 27, 29–30, 94,
  112–13, 117; odours 25
Britain x, 8, 149; and international
  politics 169; Labour governments
  in 108
B-world 32–3, 34, 35–6, 37, 38,
  40, 41; and Sherlock Holmes 35;
  see also A-world

California 60, 113; murders in
  144 n.4
capitalism 1, 6, 9–10, 14, 15–16,
  20 n.51, 78, 81, 83, 149, 159;
  agrarian 84; culture in 84; early
  14; late 2–4, 5–6, 75, 81, 98,

Pil - Compact Disc
A.T - 30 mines for money